VERY SHORT INTRODUCTIONS are for anyone wanting a stimulating and accessible way in to a new subject. They are written by experts, and have been published in more than 25 languages worldwide.

The series began in 1995, and now represents a wide variety of topics in history, philosophy, religion, science, and the humanities. Over the next few years it will grow to a library of around 200 volumes – a Very Short Introduction to everything from ancient Egypt and Indian philosophy to conceptual art and cosmology.

Very Short Introductions available now:

ANCIENT PHILOSOPHY
  Julia Annas
THE ANGLO-SAXON AGE
  John Blair
ANIMAL RIGHTS   David DeGrazia
ARCHAEOLOGY   Paul Bahn
ARCHITECTURE
  Andrew Ballantyne
ARISTOTLE   Jonathan Barnes
ART HISTORY   Dana Arnold
ART THEORY   Cynthia Freeland
THE HISTORY OF
  ASTRONOMY   Michael Hoskin
ATHEISM   Julian Baggini
AUGUSTINE   Henry Chadwick
BARTHES   Jonathan Culler
THE BIBLE   John Riches
BRITISH POLITICS
  Anthony Wright
BUDDHA   Michael Carrithers
BUDDHISM   Damien Keown
CAPITALISM   James Fulcher
THE CELTS   Barry Cunliffe
CHOICE THEORY
  Michael Allingham
CHRISTIAN ART   Beth Williamson
CLASSICS   Mary Beard and
  John Henderson
CLAUSEWITZ   Michael Howard
THE COLD WAR
  Robert McMahon

CONTINENTAL PHILOSOPHY
  Simon Critchley
COSMOLOGY   Peter Coles
CRYPTOGRAPHY
  Fred Piper and Sean Murphy
DADA AND SURREALISM
  David Hopkins
DARWIN   Jonathan Howard
DEMOCRACY   Bernard Crick
DESCARTES   Tom Sorell
DRUGS   Leslie Iversen
THE EARTH   Martin Redfern
EGYPTIAN MYTHOLOGY
  Geraldine Pinch
EIGHTEENTH-CENTURY
  BRITAIN   Paul Langford
THE ELEMENTS   Philip Ball
EMOTION   Dylan Evans
EMPIRE   Stephen Howe
ENGELS   Terrell Carver
ETHICS   Simon Blackburn
THE EUROPEAN UNION
  John Pinder
EVOLUTION
  Brian and Deborah Charlesworth
FASCISM   Kevin Passmore
THE FRENCH REVOLUTION
  William Doyle
FREUD   Anthony Storr
GALILEO   Stillman Drake
GANDHI   Bhikhu Parekh

Available soon:

For more information visit our web site

www.oup.co.uk/vsi

Paul Langford

EIGHTEENTH-CENTURY BRITAIN

A Very Short Introduction

OXFORD
UNIVERSITY PRESS

OXFORD
UNIVERSITY PRESS

Great Clarendon Street, Oxford OX2 6DP

Oxford University Press is a department of the University of Oxford.
It furthers the University's objective of excellence in research, scholarship,
and education by publishing worldwide in

Oxford New York

Auckland Bangkok Buenos Aires Cape Town Chennai
Dar es Salaam Delhi Hong Kong Istanbul Karachi Kolkata
Kuala Lumpur Madrid Melbourne Mexico City Mumbai Nairobi
São Paulo Shanghai Taipei Tokyo Toronto

Oxford is a registered trade mark of Oxford University Press
in the UK and in certain other countries

Published in the United States
by Oxford University Press Inc., New York

Text first published in *The Oxford Illustrated History of Britain* 1984
First published as a Very Short Introduction 2000

British Library Cataloguing in Publication Data
Data available

Library of Congress Cataloging in Publication Data
Data available
ISBN 978-0-19-285399-8

13 15 17 19 20 18 16 14 12

Typeset by RefineCatch Ltd, Bungay, Suffolk
Printed in Great Britain by
Ashford Colour Press Ltd, Gosport, Hampshire

Contents

List of Illustrations

The publisher and the author apologize for any errors or omissions in the above list. If contacted they will be pleased to rectify these at the earliest opportunity.

List of Maps

Chapter 1
Revolution and its Repercussions

The historical importance of the Revolution of 1688 – the 'Glorious Revolution' – has inevitably fluctuated in the process of constant reinterpretation by successive generations. It fared particularly badly at the hands of the twentieth century, and threatens to disappear altogether under the demands of modern historical scholarship. The decisive triumph of the liberal and democratic spirit, beloved of Thomas Macaulay and the Victorian Whigs, has dwindled into the conservative reaction of a selfish oligarchy. Especially when compared with modern revolutions, it seems rather to resemble a palace coup than a genuine shift of social or political power. Yet it had important and enduring consequences, not less significant than those of more spectacular convulsions. Even the relative absence of physical violence can be exaggerated. In Scotland, the supporters of the deposed king had to be crushed by force of arms, a process which was completed in 1689. In Ireland there was positively a blood-bath, one which still holds a prominent place in Irish myths and memories. When the siege of Londonderry was lifted, and James II decisively defeated at the battle of the Boyne, Ulster Protestants certainly considered their salvation to be glorious, but they can hardly have thought of it as bloodless.

Legitimizing the Illegitimate

The story might easily have been the same in England. The former royalist Nicholas L'Estrange testified that only chance, the disarray of

James II's friends, and above all the king's surprising failure to raise the royal standard in his own realm, prevented a civil war as ferocious as those of the mid-century. Yet Estrange's very relief that his family had been saved further sacrifices in the cause of the Stuarts perhaps provides a clue to the comparative tranquillity associated with the making of the revolution in England. A perceptible sense of compromise, of the need to step back from the brink, carries over the centuries from the debates of the assembly which met in London in January 1689. The Convention, which transformed itself into Parliament by the simple expedient of passing an act to that effect, displayed an understandable desire to legitimize what was manifestly illegitimate by following as far as possible the procedural forms employed at the Restoration in 1660. On matters of substance, the priority was plainly to find a common core of agreement rather than to test the more extreme solutions offered by either side. William of Orange was made king, with Mary as queen. Tories, led by Danby, would have preferred Mary as sole monarch, or some species of regency ruling technically in the name of James II. But the Protestant saviour would accept nothing less than the crown, and so it was.

Nonetheless, every effort was made to conceal the revolutionary nature of what was being done. Though James's supposedly illegal acts – particularly his reliance on a standing army and his recourse to the dispensing and suspending powers – were formally condemned, the Bill of Rights went out of its way to pretend that the deposed king had in effect abdicated, leaving a deserted realm no alternative but to seek the protection of the House of Orange. Implausible though this appeared, it was sufficient to secure the assent of a majority of the ruling class. There were, inevitably, exceptions. Some churchmen, led by Sancroft, the archbishop of Canterbury, and two of the bishops who had helped bring James II down in the Seven Bishops Case, declined to take even the cautiously worded oaths designed by the Convention. Others, like the Nottingham Tories, old champions of the court in the reaction of 1681–7, wrestled with the concept of a rightful king who owed his title to a *de facto* decision of Parliament, but not to the *de jure* ordinance of heaven.

Parliamentary Monarchy

Yet the substantive acceptance of parliamentary monarchy was achieved. The profound importance of this achievement was obscured not merely by conscious attempts to avoid dogmatic prescriptions in 1689 but by the long agonies which followed. Passive obedience and non-resistance continued to be influential concepts, buttressed as they were by elaborate arguments stressing the providential nature of the Protestant Wind in 1688, and the duty of every citizen to co-operate with any form of authority rather than submit to anarchy. For a generation, these notions continued to work on people's minds, bestowing a sense of legitimacy on the rage and despair felt by many who had seen the necessity for what had happened in 1688 but found it difficult to live with all the consequences. Beyond that, they sank into the Anglican orthodoxy of the eighteenth century and helped secure the underlying authoritarianism which was to remain an important element of political ideology in the age of the American and French Revolutions.

But, with this reservation, the major change of course carried out in 1688 can be seen to have been truly revolutionary. The Bill of Rights clearly over-rode the hereditary right which formed the basis of the restored constitution of 1660 and replaced it with the will of the nation expressed through Parliament. First William and Mary, then Mary's sister Anne, and finally, after the death of the latter's son the duke of Gloucester in 1700, the Electors of Hanover (descended from James I through the female line) all owed their title to the determination of the propertied classes. At a time when absolutism, both in theory and in practice, seemed to be in the ascendant in the Western world, the importance of this transformation should not be underestimated. Eighteenth- and nineteenth-century Whigs exaggerated the coherence and completeness of the contract theory which seemed to have triumphed in 1689 and they under-rated the tensions, contradictions, and conflicts which it entailed. But they were fundamentally correct in seeing it as a historic turning-point involving the decisive rejection of an entire conception of government.

Foreign Relations

The status of the monarchy was the conscious concern of the revolutionaries of 1688. It is doubtful whether many of them foresaw the consequences of their actions in terms of England's relations with foreign powers. In this respect, indeed, the importance of the Revolution is undenied and undeniable. Before 1688, the policy of successive rulers, Oliver Cromwell, Charles II, and James II, had been largely pro-French and anti-Dutch. After 1688 France was to become a more or less permanent enemy, and certainly a constant rival in the battle for supremacy overseas. The scale of conflict was also novel. The Nine Years War (1688–97) and the War of Spanish Succession (1702–13) involved Britain in both Continental and colonial warfare as it had not been involved since the Elizabethan struggle with Spain, and in the interim the technological and strategic complexity of warmaking had vastly increased.

The part of the English in this unexpected, if not unpredictable, consequence of the Revolution was affected by various considerations. In terms of grand strategy, the priority was to combat Louis XIV's expansionist policies in the Low Countries, and to prevent the erection of a mighty new Bourbon empire comprising the Spanish as well as French monarchy. The interests of commerce, which once had required protection against Dutch economic enterprise, could now be said to dictate an aggressive stance towards the more sustained challenge of French competition, and especially the assertion of Britain's right to a share in the trade if not the territory of the Spanish empire. These arguments were woven by the Whigs into a systematic case for an interventionist foreign policy, expressed most clearly in the Continental campaigns of William III and the duke of Marlborough. But such considerations would not have led many of the English to approve the formidable outlay of expenditure and resources in these years if it had not been for the dynastic issue. The Nine Years War has appropriately been called the War of the English Succession. William would hardly have made his armed landing at Torbay in 1688 if he had not assumed that the English alliance against France would follow logically from his own intervention in English affairs. Yet in fact diplomatic and military support from his new subjects was made much more likely by Louis XIV's imprudent championship of James II. For a while, French backing for the Jacobite camp was withdrawn when an uneasy peace was negotiated in 1697. But four years later, with the Spanish succession at stake, and Europe on the verge of war once more, it was again Louis's support for the Stuarts, this time in the shape of James's son the Old Pretender, which convinced many reluctant English people of the case for involvement in a Continental conflict.

One of the most startling aspects of the wars was the success of English arms, particularly under Marlborough in the War of Spanish Succession. It was not just that the Protestant succession was effectively secured at least for the present. More striking still was the new reputation earned by a country widely regarded as little more than a pensioner of France only a short time before. Marlborough's triumphs at Blenheim and Ramillies, not to say Sir George Rooke's at Gibraltar and James Stanhope's at Minorca, established Britain as a major force in Continental politics, a substantial power in the Mediterranean, and a worthy competitor for France overseas. The latter stages of the war, in which military progress seemed to diminish in direct proportion to national expenditure, removed the loftier ambitions suggested by the dazzling victories of the Blenheim period, but when peace was made at Utrecht in 1713 sufficient was secured to retain the essential impact of the successes, and even to create the impression of what French diplomatic historians have termed the 'English hegemony' in Europe.

Domestic Impact

Hardly less important was the domestic impact of warfare. The cost of the wars amounted to almost £150 million in an age when peacetime expenditure was thought excessive at £2 million per annum. This vast outlay required a corresponding rise in levels of taxation, with widespread political repercussions. But more interesting in retrospect is the fact that a large proportion of the bill, approximately one-third, was met by borrowing. Sums of this order could only be found in a buoyant and flexible money market, such as that created by the economic conditions of the late seventeenth century. Though land values were seriously affected by agrarian recession, trade had enjoyed a great upsurge in the 1680s and the investment surpluses released were to wash over the economy for a good many years. A post-revolution government, sorely in need of cash and prepared to mortgage the incomes of unborn generations of taxpayers to permit a competitive interest rate, offered promising investment possibilities.

The financiers whose initiative eventually led to the foundation of the Bank of England in 1694 were not, in principle, engaging in anything new. As long as wars had been undertaken, governments had been forced to rely on loans from the business community. What was new was the political infrastructure which was necessitated by the exceptionally heavy borrowing of this period. The credit-worthiness of the new regime, based as it was on a parliamentary title, depended on without the clear understanding that the propertied classes would ultimately be prepared to foot the bill. Without a matching recognition on the part of the regime that it must closely collaborate with those classes and their representatives, no such understanding could exist. The National Debt and all it entailed was built on this essential nexus of interest linking an illegitimate dynasty, the financial world, and the taxpaying public.

As war followed war and decade followed decade the burden of debt grew. Successive governments found it ever harder to avoid borrowing, and the main function of those taxes which were raised was often merely to pay the interest charges on the debt. With hindsight, the advantages of this system, without precise parallel in contemporary Europe, are obvious. The political security of an otherwise somewhat shaky regime was enhanced, and national resources in wartime boosted by this machinery for channelling private wealth into public expenditure. At the time, the disadvantages attracted more attention. The pretence that the National Debt could actually be repaid and the nation released from the threat of bankruptcy became increasingly thin. The anxieties of a society traditionally ill-disposed to taxation in general and new forms of taxation in particular made the task of the Treasury and the Committee of Ways and Means increasingly harrowing.

Yet, even at the time, there were those who had a shrewd perception of one quite priceless political advantage of the new system. This arose from its impact on Parliament, and especially on the House of Commons. For everything depended on Parliament's part in this elaborate process, and Parliament was understandably jealous of its rights in matters of finance. The land tax, the basic guarantee of the taxpayer's commitment to the National Debt, was cautiously voted for a year at a time. Even the customs and excise duties, granted for much longer periods, were extended and renewed only after the most prolonged debate and haggling. The 'budget' was nominally an achievement of the mid-century, when the term was first used during Henry Pelham's time as first lord of the Treasury (1743–54). But its essential features can be traced back to the Revolution, and it is this aspect of 1689 which more than anything else finally secured Parliament's central place in constitutional development.

At times in the seventeenth century it had been possible to see the legislature as a faintly absurd and decidedly irritating survival of England's medieval past, an irrational obstruction to efficient monarchical government which might profitably be dispensed with altogether. Now its future was secure; since 1689 Parliament has met for a substantial period every year. In this sense the Revolution gave a novel twist to an old problem: eighteenth-century politicians asked themselves not how to do away with the need for Parliament, or even how to crush it. Rather they had to consider how to manipulate it. The arts of management were to provide the key to the conduct of Georgian politics.

The Church

It was impossible in the late seventeenth century to engage in political revolution without raising the prospect or the spectre (depending on one's viewpoint) of ecclesiastical revolution. In this respect the Revolution of 1688 was perhaps important not merely for what it did but for what it failed to do. Many contemporaries hoped for a radical revision of the Church settlement of the 1660s. There was talk of a truly comprehensive national Church, and for some dissenters, particularly the Presbyterians, the possibilities of reconcilation to the establishment seemed stronger than at any time since the Hampton Court conference in 1604. In the event, however, their hopes were dashed. As in 1662 the Anglican squirearchy would permit no weakening of the hierarchical and episcopalian structure of the Church. It would be inappropriate to talk of a Laudian or high-church reaction at this time. But any sign of genuine *rapprochement* with the dissenters was quickly extinguished. Instead, the latter were offered the least that could be offered against the background of recent events, a grudging toleration. The Toleration Act of 1689 in effect granted freedom of worship to Protestant nonconformists in premises licensed by Anglican bishops, provided that those concerned shared the basic doctrines laid down in the Thirty-nine Articles and sanctioned by the Act of Uniformity. This seemed a far cry from the prospect held out to dissenters of all kinds by James II.

No doubt for this reason, it has been customary to play down the full significance of the Toleration Act. A qualified liberty permitted to those whose beliefs were defined in qualified terms seemed a poor reward for men who had resisted the temptations offered by the Declarations of Indulgence and had welcomed William of Orange. But such judgements depend heavily on the point of view. For dissenters who had been vigorously persecuted as recently as the early 1680s, the Toleration Act provided an unprecedented statutory security. From the vantage point of anxious churchmen it was no less important to maintain the substance of the Restoration Settlement. The Prayer Book of 1662 was to remain the liturgical basis of Anglican worship until the twentieth century; but in 1689 it seemed to offer a precarious platform of doctrine without which established Protestantism might be lost.

Paradoxically, the resulting exclusiveness of the Church had much to do with England's eighteenth-century reputation as a civilized society in a barbarous world. A comprehensive national Church embracing all but a small number of sectaries and papists would have been a very different matter from a restricted religious establishment, co-existing with large numbers of nonconformists. The difference was perhaps a tolerant, pluralist society. The legal recognition of liberty of worship went far beyond what had been achieved in most of Europe, and Voltaire was to hold it up as the crucial element in the development of a free polity. If so, it was to a large extent the consequence of the Revolution.

The achievements of these years had a price in the social tensions and political conflicts which marked the Augustan era. Pre-eminent among the signs of strain was indeed the plight of the religious establishment. The great cry of the period was 'The Church in Danger'. Whether it was truly in danger seems doubtful in retrospect. Toleration was obviously a fearful blow to those who dreamed of reviving a Laudian church. But the swelling tide of latitudinarian theology and sentiment made it seem innocuous enough to most. Moreover, the political monopoly enjoyed by Anglicans under the Test and Corporation Acts was left intact by the Revolution Settlement. Here, however, was the rub. For in practice there was every indication that dissenters were able to challenge and evade

1. The Church in danger. This design for a fan, of 1711, glorifies Dr Sacheverell, shown here with the six bishops who supported him at his trial, and other Anglican heroes, including the Marian martyrs. On the left the Church of England is protected by the queen and by Providence. On the right the dangers of republicanism and popery are displayed

this monopoly. The readiness of many nonconformists to resort to occasional conformity, annually taking the sacraments according to the Anglican rite in order to meet the requirements of the statutes, and for the rest worshipping in their own meeting houses, was a constant source of irritation to their enemies. Whether the actual practice of occasional conformity grew in this period is uncertain. But it was unquestionably more noticeable now that dissenting chapels were publicly recognized, and now that the double standard apparently observed by those who attended them was plain to all.

Moreover, the general climate of the 1690s and 1700s provoked anxiety and even hysteria on the part of churchmen. Theological speculation and deistic tendencies were much discussed and much feared. John Toland's *Christianity Not Mysterious*, one of the earliest and most systematic attempts to popularize the case for 'natural' against 'revealed' religion, began a torrent of polemical debate on such matters in 1697. Nor did it help that some of the worst offenders were themselves clergy of the established Church. Samuel Clarke, the Whig sceptic whose assault on Trinitarianism brought the wrath of

Convocation upon his head in 1712, and Benjamin Hoadly, who held three bishoprics in succession but denied the divine nature both of his office and of the Church itself, were only the more spectacular examples of the heretical spirit which seemed to mark the progress of the early Enlightenment in England.

Party Politics

The high-church reaction to these trends reached its peak under Queen Anne when the presence on the throne of a pious and theologically conservative queen provided an additional impulse. But its force derived much from other developments, many of them connected with party politics. The Tories, who frequently described themselves as 'The Church party', depended greatly for their appeal on the sense of crisis in the Church. They also drew extensively on the emotional support of the backwoods Anglican squirearchy. For the latter, the world opened up by the Revolution brought nothing but ill. The wars of the period necessitated the heaviest direct taxation since the 1650s. A land tax of four shillings in the pound came as a heavy burden on estates already afflicted by agricultural depression. Moreover, the war for which such sacrifices were required seemed designed to benefit precisely the enemies of the gentry – the merchants, manufacturers, and above all 'moneyed men' most active in the commercial and financial expansion of late Stuart England. Such men, it seemed, were often religious dissenters, escaped all but indirect taxes, and invariably pursued Whig politics.

The link between the old and new party systems was sometimes tenuous. The new Tories of Anne's reign were often drawn from families with a Puritan or Whiggish background; their leader, Robert Harley, was himself one such. On the other side, the Whig Junto, whose ruthless pursuit of place and power earned them an unenviable reputation for placing party before principle, seemed unlikely descendants of the Country Whigs of 1679. But there was no doubt about the intensity of party feeling in the early eighteenth century. It reached its height in 1710 when the Whigs impeached the Tory divine, Dr Sacheverell, for preaching the old doctrine of non-resistance. The popular convulsions which followed clearly revealed the potential for political instability which the Revolution had incidentally created.

The Triennial Act of 1694 had principally been designed to compel the Crown to summon Parliament regularly, in which respect it proved unnecessary. But it also provided for frequent elections, and the consequence was a period of the most intense and unremitting electoral conflict, involving 10 general elections in 20 years and exceeding anything which had gone before. Moreover, the effective abolition of State censorship, with the lapsing of the Licensing Act in 1695, ensured a large and growing forum for public debate. It is no coincidence that these years witnessed the decisive stage in the establishment of Grub Street, in the emergence of the periodical press, and in the growth of a genuinely popular political audience.

In general, the reign of Anne has been seen by historians as the natural backdrop to the achievement of political stability. But on the evidence available to contemporaries it seemed rather to suggest that the price of limited monarchy and financial security was political chaos.

Chapter 2
The Rise of Robinocracy

The Hanoverian Accession in 1714 brought new tensions to an already strained situation. While Anne lived, it had been possible, in terms of sentiment if not of logic, to consider her as a true Stuart occupying the throne in some sense in trust for her family. With the arrival of a German-speaking Elector of Hanover, strongly committed to intervention abroad and Whiggism at home, such pretences became difficult to sustain. From a dynastic standpoint everything was to play for in 1714. Many urged the Pretender to consider that London was worth the abandonment of the mass; had James III returned to the Anglican fold he would plainly have strengthened the chances of a second Stuart Restoration. Without this personal sacrifice, the Jacobite rebellion of 1715 proved a damp squib. France, after the death of Louis XIV in the same year, was in no position to involve itself in English adventures. Even in Scotland, where the rebellion had its seat and indeed its heart, the prospects for the Stuarts were not particularly promising. The Scottish Union, concluded in 1708 in an atmosphere of considerable urgency, had taken much of the sting out of the succession problem. Many Scots mourned the loss of their national Parliament and thereby their independence. But the Union was shrewdly designed to preserve Scottish legal and ecclesiastical institutions, while simultaneously offering real commercial benefits through incorporation in England's imperial system. In these circumstances, the failure of the '15 was to all intents and purposes a foregone conclusion. If the Old

Pretender missed his chance, so in a different sense did his apparently successful rival, George I.

The New Regime

By the latter part of Anne's reign, the unpopularity of the war, the electoral appeal of the 'Church in Danger', and not least the queen's own irritation with the Junto Whigs had placed the Tories firmly in the saddle. For most of them the interests of the established Church took precedence over sentimental attachment to the Stuart dynasty. A judiciously bipartisan policy on the part of the new regime, on the lines of William III's tactics in 1689, would have done much to ease the transition of 1714. Instead, George I displayed all too clearly his readiness to make the Hanoverian succession the exclusive property of the Whigs. The years 1714–21 witnessed a campaign for Whiggish dominance which comprehensively alienated the Tories, made the dangers of the Jacobite rebellion greater than they need have been, and generally threatened to reshape the Revolution settlement.

First the Septennial Act was passed, ensuring that the new Whig government would not have to face an unmanageable electorate until the greater part of its work was complete. It was rumoured that, when that time came, the Whigs would remove all statutory restraints on the duration of Parliaments, making possible the revival of 'long' or 'pensioner' Parliaments. At the same time, the means by which the Tories of Anne's reign had endeavoured to shackle dissent, the Occasional Conformity and Schism Acts, were first suspended and then in 1718 repealed altogether. A Universities Bill was designed to give the Crown complete control of Fellowships and Scholarships in Oxford and Cambridge, with a view to transforming the principal nurseries of the Church and the professions into Whig preserves. Above all the Peerage Bill of 1719 was projected to restrict the House of Lords to approximately its existing size. This would have ensured permanent Whig hegemony in the Upper House, regardless of any change of mind on the part of the monarch, and provided the Whigs with a built-in check on legislation affecting their interests. With this programme there went a steady, systematic purge of Tories in the lord-lieutenancies and commissions of the peace, in the armed forces, and in the civil service at all levels.

Complete success in this great enterprise would have created a system much like that which emerged in Sweden at this time, and which condemned that country to 50 years of national impotence and aristocratic factionalism. It would have established an oligarchy as unlimited as that absolute monarchy which generations in seventeenth-century England had so dreaded. It would also have made virtually impossible one of the eighteenth century's most characteristic achievements, a stable yet flexible political structure. That it failed owed much to the divisions among the Whigs themselves. Their plans proceeded relatively smoothly while the great Whig families united to crush their opponents during the early years of George I's reign. But this union proved short-lived.

The new king's foreign policy caused severe strains by its blatant use of England's naval power to secure Hanover's Baltic ambitions. There was also an increasingly bitter struggle for pre-eminence within the ministry. The eventual result, in 1717, was the Whig split, which placed Walpole and Townshend in opposition and left Stanhope and Sunderland more firmly ensconced at court than ever. Palace politics were also subject to upheaval. The king's son, the future George II, and his wife Princess Caroline clearly indicated their intention of siding with Townshend and thereby began a long tradition of political intrigue by Hanoverian heirs to the throne. In this situation there was little hope of completing the grandiose plans of Stanhope for the promised land of Whiggism. In the House of Commons Walpole himself played a leading part in defeating the Peerage Bill and forcing the abandonment of the Universities Bill. Any hope the ministry had of saving something from the wreckage of their plans was lost soon after in the South Sea Bubble.

The South Sea Bubble

In retrospect, there is a certain inevitability about the South Sea Bubble and the general financial crash which went with it. It seems to bring to a fitting conclusion the intense and inflated commercialism which had accompanied the rise of the 'moneyed interest' in the preceding years. Yet initially there was much to be said for the scheme which caused this convulsion. The financial interests represented in the Bank of England had enjoyed a more than favourable return on their investments during the wars, and there was obviously room for greater competition between the nation's creditors. The Tory ministers of Queen Anne's reign had indeed encouraged the formation of the South Sea Company in 1711 with a view to providing an effective alternative to the Whig Bank. Moreover, there was little doubt that the funds existed, not merely in the City, but among smaller savers generally, for a more extended and more equitable investment in the public debt. The South Sea Company's scheme of 1719 seemed well calculated to redistribute the National Debt while offering better terms to the national Exchequer.

The difficulties began not with the essential logic of the scheme but with the many and varied interests involved in it. For the directors of the Company, and especially the inner group which initiated the project, there was the need to make a substantial profit not merely for themselves but for the many courtiers, ministers, and MPs whose support was politically essential to secure acceptance of their proposals. That support was bought at a high price in terms of stock supplied on favourable terms, or even stock granted by way of open bribery. In short, many of those involved in the management of the South Sea Scheme had a strong interest in quick profits, which could only be achieved by boosting the Company's potential far beyond competing investment possibilities.

Such an exercise depended on the attractions of the Company's trade in the south seas. The Anglo-Spanish treaty of 1713 had given the Company a monopoly of the Spanish slave trade and a valuable share in the Spanish American market for European goods. In theory, this offered the most promising prospects. In practice, the difficulties of managing this far-flung trade from London were to prove immense, and they were not rendered less by the often bitter conflicts between the British and Spanish governments. The trade could not have proved profitable in the short run, and even with time it could hardly fulfil the wild expectations raised in 1719. But realities were quickly forgotten in the mania for speculation which prevailed in the early months of 1720. Provided the stock was rising, new speculators were constantly encouraged to invest, permitting those who had already purchased to unload their holdings at a handsome profit. The constant inflow of funds justified new issues of stock and increasingly vociferous assertions of the durability of the investment, not to say still more generous pay-offs to the politicians. In this situation, created by a corrupt regime, a naive investing public, and a well-established National Debt, the inevitable happened.

The Bubble grew steadily, encouraging still more fraudulent bubbles in ever more implausible projects as it grew. When confidence eventually failed and the bubble burst the consequences were catastrophic, particularly for those who had sold substantial assets in land or other forms of property to buy at absurdly inflated prices. Little could be done for these sufferers, by no means drawn only from the wealthiest classes. Parliament rushed through a statute severely restricting joint-stock companies for the future, but this was shutting the stable door after the horse had bolted. More dramatic action was needed to minimize the damage to the regime. The king and the Prince of Wales were publicly reconciled. The opposition Whigs were welcomed back into office, Townshend to set about cultivating the goodwill of the king's mistress the duchess of Kendal, Walpole to push through the Commons a solution for the Bubble crisis which would at least protect the National Debt and save the face of the court.

In this task, which earned him an enduring reputation for 'screening' corruption and fraud in high places, Walpole was in one sense aided by the very gravity of the situation. Many of those implicated in the murky transactions of 1720 were Tories who had no more enthusiasm than their Whig counterparts for public exposure. Moreover the Bubble was part of an international crisis with matching disasters in Paris and Amsterdam; it was not implausible to lay some of the blame on impersonal financial forces unconnected with individuals in the City or at court. In any event the king's ministers were, with the exception of two or three suitable scapegoats, permitted to get away with their crimes. For Walpole all this represented a great political triumph, fittingly capped by the fortuitous elimination of his rivals. Within two years, both Stanhope and Sunderland had died, leaving the way open for a new era of Walpolian supremacy, or as his opponents were to term it 'Robinocracy'.

Sickness and Death

Contemporaries, of course, could not be expected to foresee the relative stability which lay ahead. The 1720s were troubled years, not least in the most basic terms of human health and survival. The decade began, not merely with the Bubble, but with fears of a visitation from the plague which was currently devastating the south of France and which could readily have been transmitted to London by way of Marseilles and the shipping lanes. In the event, the panic proved unjustified; the strains of the disease which had periodically ravaged so much of Europe since the first onset of the Black Death nearly four hundred years earlier were approaching dormancy if not extinction. But this was not obvious at the time and in any case there were less exotic, home-grown maladies which continued to exert a tenacious hold on the vital statistics of demography.

The later 1720s were particularly harrowing in this respect. The first three years of George II's reign, which began in 1727, were afflicted by successive waves of smallpox and influenza-like infections, imprecisely and variously described by contemporaries as agues and fevers. The demographic consequences were serious. Much of the slow and slender gain in population which had occurred since the 1670s seems to have been wiped out in what was evidently the worst mortality crisis since the 1580s. By 1731 the total population stood at about 5,200,000, a figure probably lower than that for Cromwell's England in the mid-1650s.

Corruption and Crime

The sense of sickness which pervaded the period was more than physiological. The greed, fraudulence, and hysteria which had characterized the South Sea Bubble were denounced both in the press and from the pulpit as the ruling vices of the years which followed. Luxury and lavish living were seen as the causes, moral decay and dissolution as the consequences.

There seemed to be striking evidence of this in the great scandals which disfigured public life at this time. A whole series of parliamentary investigations uncovered extensive corruption in high places. The trustees of the Derwentwater estates were found to have connived at the sale of forfeited Jacobite property to some of their own number at artificially low prices. The directors and officials of the Charitable Corporation, whose duty it was to provide employment and assistance for the poor, were convicted of jobbery, misappropriation, and even outright peculation. In both cases, prominent MPs and supporters of the government were implicated. More sensational still was the impeachment of the Lord Chancellor, Lord Macclesfield, for organizing the sale of judicial offices. Even his ministerial colleagues declined to defend him when it emerged that this flourishing branch of commercial law had been financed from the proceeds of private property entrusted to the care of Chancery. That the guardians of equity should thus be caught in the act of infringing it seemed peculiarly shocking to an age which entertained a profound respect for rights of property.

Moreover, public misdeeds could readily be matched by private ones. Crime, a distorting mirror of society, but a mirror nonetheless, seemed to become ever more organized, more commercial, and more cynical. Jonathan Wild, the master thief-taker, was a fitting representative of his time. Most of his profits were gained by restoring to their owners the goods stolen by his own minions. His success depended on the corrupt collaboration of JPs and their officers in the metropolis. His was only one growth sector in the flourishing economy of crime. Poachers in the royal forests were often well-organized, systematic suppliers to the London market. The smugglers of the south and east coasts pursued market principles and economies of scale, again with the frequent co-operation of officials and the public at large.

The authorities made somewhat desperate attempts to combat these threats. Wild was brought to justice on a technicality. His execution in 1725 was to ensure his place in popular mythology. The poachers of Windsor Forest and elsewhere were the subject of new legislation, the draconian Black Act of 1723. They had to wait until the twentieth century to achieve the status of folk-heroes, in their case bestowed by historians intent on treating them as authentic representatives of a popular culture. The smugglers seemed to flourish almost in proportion to the government's efforts to suppress them; at their most active in the 1730s they were capable of mounting pitched battles with George II's dragoons in their heroic service to a consumer society.

Satire and Polemic

For this was what was emerging in early Hanoverian England. In this respect the South Sea Bubble is best seen not as the grand finale of post-Revolution England, but rather as a spectacular curtain-raiser to the prosperity, vulgarity, and commercialism of the mid-eighteenth century. The theatrical metaphor is peculiarly appropriate, for the period has a special significance in the history of the performing arts. The 1720s and 1730s witnessed a considerable expansion in the London theatre and an increasingly political role for it. Until the court took action to obtain extensive powers of censorship in 1737 it was the forum, along with the press generally, for a mounting campaign of criticism of the kind of society which seemed to have emerged during and after the Bubble.

Nothing expressed such criticism more effectively than John Gay's *Beggar's Opera*, the great success of 1728. Whether the opera was actually intended as a political satire is uncertain, but it is significant of the contemporary climate of opinion that it was instantly accepted as such. Gay's message fitted well into the prevailing concern with illusion and unreality. It clearly depicted the court of George II as a kind of thieves' kitchen; the morality of the ruling class was put on a par with that of the London underworld. It was a point which Fielding was to reinforce by means of his unflattering comparison of Jonathan Wild with Sir Robert Walpole. It also had closely matching themes in Pope's *Dunciad*, Swift's *Gulliver's Travels*, and Bolingbroke's *Craftsman*, all products of a remarkable decade of polemical satire. Many of its elements were familiar ones: the retreat into classicism, the appeal to country values, the attraction of the rural idyll, above all the incessant criticism of the supposedly synthetic, moneyed world of early eighteenth-century commercialism. In these respects the literary and journalistic invective of the Walpole era can be seen, indeed, as the final, most violent surge of a tide which had been flowing for many years. But in inspiration for the future, or constructive analysis of alternative possibilities, it was manifestly deficient.

The Rise of Walpole

When Gay's audience glimpsed in Macheath the very essence of Walpolian politics, they seized upon one of the most significant aspects of the period – the close connection, seen if not established, between the political character of the Hanoverian regime and the supposed ills of contemporary society. With a few exceptions (notably the cartoonist

William Hogarth, who reserved most of his energies for satirizing manners and morals), the intellectual and artistic elite of London was remarkably unanimous in its view that Walpole was the arch-villain of the piece. His characteristic image was that of a *parvenu* Norfolk placeman, enriched by a career of systematic corruption (he had been prosecuted by the Tories for official peculation in 1712) and elevated to supreme power for his lack of principle and submission to the views of the court. Before 1727, his brother-in-law, Lord Townshend, had shared both his power and his unpopularity. But the death of George I and the accession of a new king placed him in the full glare of public attention. By his adroit management of George II and more especially Queen Caroline, Walpole elbowed out all rivals for power, including, in 1730, Townshend himself. As a result he soon achieved a lonely eminence such as none had enjoyed, perhaps, since Danby in the 1670s. It was doubtless enhanced by the personal unpopularity of the king himself, who made no secret of his preference for German surroundings and company, and who made no attempt to boost his standing with popular opinion in Britain.

Walpole's hegemony inevitably drew the full fire of Grub Street on his personal position. He was the Great Man, the English Colossus, the Man Mountain. He also appeared as the perfect representative of the politics of illusion – the Norfolk trickster, the Savoy Rareeshowman, Palinurus the magician, Merlin the wizard, the Screenmaster-General. Both his mastery of the irascible and unpredictable George II and his control of a previously unmanageable Parliament were portrayed in countless broadsides and prints as the arts of a veritable political conjuror.

The basis of Walpole's success at the time and ever since, has been traced to his skilful use of influence and even bribery. The stability which seems to mark the period and to separate it from the political chaos of earlier years can be viewed, on this reading, as the natural culmination of forces working in favour of the executive. The expansion of government as a result of the wars, especially the vast machinery created to operate the new financial system, generated a considerable quantity of new patronage. Moreover, the overwhelming necessity for post-revolution governments to obtain a working majority in the Commons provided a strong incentive to use this patronage for the purposes of parliamentary management. Hence the emergence of a much larger, much more disciplined Court and Treasury party, capable of bridging the ancient gap between Crown and Commons and inaugurating a new era of harmony between executive and legislature.

It is an attractive theory, but not all the premisses are secure and not all the conclusions inescapable. Walpole's principles of management were far from novel. At least since the reign of Charles II, they had been employed by successive ministers to maintain a substantial court party in the House of Commons. Placemanship and careerism, not to say widespread evidence of corruption, had marked the reign of Anne as much as that of her successors. In some respects, indeed, the peaceful years of Walpole's ministry reduced the amount of patronage available. It is true enough that both Walpole himself and his effective successor Henry Pelham were adroit managers, and that both welded the court party into an exceptionally efficient instrument of control. But it needed more than patronage to create the classical parliamentary system of Georgian England.

This is not to deny Walpole's own inimitable talents. As a courtier he was without compare. His manipulation of the queen and (partly through her) of the king was a consummate mixture of flattery, cajolery, and bullying, brilliantly described in the memoirs of Lord Hervey, whose intimacy with Queen Caroline gave him ample opportunity to witness it. But winning courtiers were nothing new. What was more striking was the unusual combination of gifts which permitted him to handle MPs with equal skill.

His decision to remain in the House of Commons as first minister was quite critical in this respect. Where previous ministers had traditionally

Designed by the Author of Common Sense.   Publish'd according to Act of Parliament 1731.   Price 1.ˢ

2. The politics of Robinocracy. Political cartoons of the Walpole era were crude but effective. (*Above*): Walpole (with wand) and Queen Caroline are shown using a magical potion to control the irascible George II, in the guise of satyr. (*Facing*): The Broad Bottom or coalition ministry which succeeded Walpole shows what it thinks of pledges to reduce taxation and crush corruption. The prints incidentally reveal the limited development of personal caricature at this time; neither Walpole in the print above nor Sir John Hynde Cotton, the Tory leader in the centre of the print on the right, displays anything like a physical resemblance to the subject

departed to the Lords, Walpole made a point of remaining in the chamber which ultimately controlled the purse-strings of government. As a debater he was somewhat crude (not necessarily a disadvantage), skilled, and extremely effective. As a conciliator, his capacity for ascertaining and implementing the views of the typical country gentleman was outstanding. But most important of all were his policies, which differed profoundly from the partisan programme of his old Whig colleagues. His desire to avoid exacerbating ancient animosities was particularly marked in his treatment of the Church. With the assistance of Indemnity Acts, the dissenters were left to enjoy their freedom of worship and even some measure of local power. But there was no

serious attempt to break the Anglican monopoly in principle, and the repeal of the Test and Corporation Acts had to wait another hundred years. Nor was there any serious talk of wholesale changes elsewhere, in the corporations, the universities, or indeed Parliament itself. The new Whig policy of peace with France became under Walpole a policy of peace with everyone, carrying with it the priceless advantage of low taxation.

In theory the Whig supremacy continued unabated. In practice Walpole subtly transformed the basis of the Hanoverian regime. The politics of coercion gave way to those of consensus; the objective of an exclusive oligarchy was replaced by the uninspiring but solid appeal of a ruling coalition open to anyone prepared to pay lip-service to undefined 'Revolution principles'.

Patronage and Stability

Even without Walpole the Hanoverian regime would eventually have had an important impact on the pattern of politics. For simply in terms of corruption it was not the novelty of Walpole's management which counted, but rather the extent to which patronage was channelled in one direction. Before 1714, uncertain or inconsistent policies on the part of the court had made the calculations of placemen and patrons exceedingly difficult. From the boroughmonger at the apex of the electoral pyramid to the humble exciseman or common councillor at its base, it was far from clear where the means to profit and power lay. Much of the instability of party politics under Queen Anne arose from the resulting oscillations. After 1715 this problem was resolved for more than a generation by one simple and central fact of public life. Both George I and George II objected to the inclusion of Tories in their ministries, and with the exception of the short-lived Broad Bottom Administration in 1743, a product of the instability which followed Walpole's fall, the Tory party remained in the wilderness for more than 40 years.

Paradoxically, this proscription made ministerial stability more secure. Court Tories were more determinedly courtiers than they were Tories, and the prospect of permanent exclusion from place and profit was more than many could bear. Moreover, Walpole's form of Whiggism was undemanding and there were many whose families had previously sided with the Tories who found little difficulty in subscribing to the new Whig principles. This particularly was the case with those who from interest or instinct gravitated naturally towards the politics of courts. By the 1730s the close boroughs of Cornwall, divided between Whigs and Tories at the beginning of the century, were dependable Whig preserves. In the Lords only a handful of Tory peers continued loyal to their friends in the Commons, though in 1712 Harley had achieved a Tory majority there. The change was not sudden or spectacular but it was steady and sustained, and some of the most important political names of the eighteenth century were part of it, including both the Pitt and the Fox families.

There were somewhat similar developments in Scotland and Ireland. Moving Scotland's politicians to Westminster opened up for them a whole new field of patronage. Simultaneously it gave London's politicians a powerful incentive to assist them. Whigs north and south of the border benefited correspondingly. Ireland had not lost its Parliament but in practice rarely challenged the supremacy of Westminster. The Crown's supporters in London and Dublin worked for the most part in harmony. In Ireland's case most of the patronage that oiled the wheels of government was paid for by the Irish themselves. There were other differences between the Scottish and Irish cases. In Scotland the most threatening resentment was that of the defeated Jacobites. In Ireland, though an alienated Catholic peasantry far outnumbered Protestants, it was that of discontented Whig 'patriots'.

The stability of the political scene under Walpole and Pelham was a major achievement of the Hanoverian system; but it is important not to exaggerate its extent. Politics in George II's reign did not descend into the torpor with which they are often associated. For the price of Hanoverian identification with Whiggism, albeit a somewhat watery Whiggism, was the permanent alienation of the die-hard 'country' Tory families. These families, though they rarely produced politicians of the first rank, maintained a certain resilience in opposition and provided an important focus for other potentially hostile elements. They made life difficult and unpleasant for those of their comrades who did defect; for example, when one of their aristocratic leaders, Earl Gower, joined Henry Pelham, the result at the general election of 1747 was rioting of almost unparalleled ferocity in Gower's home county of Staffordshire. In the counties, indeed, the Tories had their heartland. Among the 40-shilling freeholders of the county electorates, particularly in the Midlands, the west country, and Wales, they received consistent and

3. Latitudinarian learning. A typical charity school at Burrough Green, Cambridgeshire, founded in 1708 by the rector of the village. The schoolmaster, for whom accommodation was included, was required 'diligently and faithfully [to] teach and instruct in reading of the Holy Bible and in writing a fair hand and in arithmetic the Children of the poorest and of other inhabitants of Burrough Green'

even increasing support. Elsewhere they were influential if not dominating. The Toryism of the Church was bound to be diluted by the persistent drip of Whig jobbery, but one of the great seminaries of the Church, the university of Oxford, remained loyal to the Anglican gentry, and there was sufficient ecclesiastical patronage in the hands of the Tory families to maintain a powerful interest. In substantial cities there were also promising reservoirs of potential opposition to the regime. In London, Bristol, Norwich, and Newcastle, for instance, there was a long tradition of popular participation in politics, and much combustible material for Tory incendiaries. The Walpole system was too widely based to be considered a narrow oligarchy, but while a significant portion of the landed and clerical classes and a large body of middle- and lower-class opinion in the towns opposed it, the stability of the age could be more apparent than real.

The Regime at Risk

Naturally enough, the conditions for genuine crisis were created only when the regime itself was divided. By the early 1730s Walpole was faced by a dangerous alliance of rivals at court. Their opportunity came with his celebrated attempt to extend the excise system, a project which was financially sound but which awakened the deepest and most violent antipathy among those numerous English people who detested new taxes and feared the expansion of the government's bureaucracy. Only Walpole's readiness to withdraw his scheme in 1733 and the solid support of George II against his court rivals saved his administration; even so, the general election of 1734 produced a wide-spread reaction against him and a severely reduced majority in the House of Commons.

An even more serious situation arose four years later. The powerful out-of-doors agitation which demanded an aggressive stance towards the Spanish Empire in 1738 and 1739 was all the more dangerous because it had support from Frederick Prince of Wales. The consequent alliance of alienated Tories, discontented Whigs, hostile business men, popular politicians, and the heir to the throne was dangerous indeed and eventually it was not only to force Walpole into a war which he profoundly disliked, but even to bring him down in 1742. The problem of the reversionary interest was particularly alarming; it was, until Frederick's death in 1751, to pose Pelham the same problems which it posed Walpole.

Even without these internal strains, the Whig supremacy faced considerable opposition. The Jacobite threat was probably exaggerated; it may be doubted whether many of those who toasted 'the king over the water' would actually have risked either their property or their lives for the House of Stuart. Theirs was a protest rather of emblematic drinking glass and buckler than of musket and bayonet. Nonetheless, the more committed among them had some encouragement. The War of Austrian Succession (1740–8) found Britain involved, not merely against Spain overseas, but against a powerful Bourbon coalition on the Continent. In that war George II seemed primarily concerned to protect his beloved electorate; the consequent clash with domestic interests, and above all the unpopularity of investing British money and British blood in Germany and the Netherlands, gave patriot politicians ample ammunition for attacks on the regime.

Walpole had predicted long before that warfare would mean a struggle for the English succession on English soil, and so it proved. When the Jacobite invasion came in 1745, it revealed the full extent of the danger to the Hanoverian dynasty. By European standards, the British standing army was tiny; even the small and ill-assorted force which the Young Pretender brought into the heart of the English Midlands in December 1745 plainly stretched the defenders to the limit. An effective militia, without Tory support, had long since been abandoned; many of the country gentry offered at best sullen neutrality. The ferocious terror which was deployed against the Scottish Highlanders after the Jacobite army had been pushed back and finally crushed at Culloden was a measure of the alarm and even panic which had gripped the authorities in London. In these respects, as in others, the crisis of 1745 provides a useful corrective to excessively bland portrayals of the essential complacency of the Whig system. The customary picture of political apathy and aristocratic elegance can be a misleading one. It hardly fits the ragged but bloody progress of the rebels in 1745, nor do the relatively sedate years of the early 1750s altogether bear it out. Pelham, for example, whose adroit management had steered his country safely if somewhat ignominiously out of the war and whose financial acumen put the National Debt on a more secure basis thereafter, proved capable of misjudging the political climate. His Jew Bill of 1753, designed to soften the civil disabilities of the Jewish community in Britain, provoked a torrent of high-church hostility and intolerance and compelled him to repeal the offending measure before he could be punished for it in the general election of 1754. Again, the Jacobite alarms and excursions were far from over. As late as 1753 London was regaled with the spectacle of a Jacobite rebel being publicly hanged; in some respects, no doubt, politics in the eighteenth century was more polite, but it was not invariably so.

Chapter 3
Industry and Idleness

The death throes of Jacobitism coincided chronologically with the passing away of pre-industrial society, for older accounts of the immense economic growth and change described as the industrial revolution locate its birth firmly in the mid-eighteenth century. Yet the period which in retrospect seems to have provided the platform for industrial take-off was widely regarded at the time as one of worrying recession, and continues to present problems of evaluation.

In the 1730s and 1740s agricultural prices were exceptionally low; some important manufacturing regions, particularly the old textile centres, suffered serious unemployment and unrest. But there were also more promising developments. Low food prices permitted higher spending on consumer goods and thereby encouraged the newer industries, particularly in the Midlands. If agriculture was frequently depressed by these prices it was also stimulated by them, in East Anglia for example, to increase production. The improved techniques of mixed farming often associated with the age of 'Turnip' Townshend do not belong exclusively to this period, but their importance was certainly more widely appreciated.

Turnpike Roads

In other sectors there was very marked advance. For instance, the 1730s witnessed one of the most striking developments in the history of transport – the construction of a nation-wide turnpike system. Before 1730, only a handful of turnpike trusts had been established. Most main roads, including the Great North Road beyond Northamptonshire and almost the whole of the Great West Road, depended for their maintenance on those unfortunate parishes which happened to lie in the immediate vicinity. The roads of early Georgian England, subjected to the immense strain of rapidly growing passenger traffic and ever more burdensome freight services between major centres of consumption, were rightly considered a national disgrace. Turnpike trusts were a neat, if not always popular, solution, which permitted the injection of substantial sums of locally raised capital into repair and maintenance, on the security of a carefully graduated system of tolls.

The heyday of the trusts lay in the four middle decades of the century. They testified strongly to the vitality of the provinces, with a large proportion of the new roads in the north and in the West Midlands; by 1770, when the canals were beginning to offer stiff competition for freight, they offered a genuinely national network of relatively efficient transport. The effect on journey times was dramatic. Provincial centres such as York, Manchester, and Exeter were well over three days' travel from London in the 1720s; by 1780 they could be reached in not much more than 24 hours. These reductions, which applied to almost all important routes, seem to have stretched contemporary transport technology to the limit; they were subject to little further improvement until about 1820, when John McAdam and Thomas Telford were to achieve further striking savings.

The development of the turnpikes would not have been possible without a great expansion of inland consumption, trade, and capital. But the internal growth implied in these years was more than matched by expansion overseas. Again contemporary appearances could be misleading. Patriot politicians continued to hold before the public an essentially old-fashioned view of empire. Colonies still tended to be seen primarily as valuable sources of raw materials, as dumping grounds

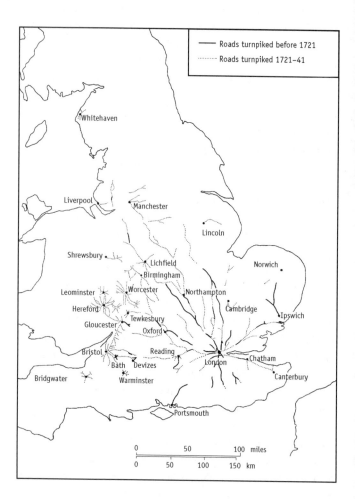

Whitehaven

Liverpool

Manchester

Lincoln

Shrewsbury

Lichfield

Birmingham

Norwich

Leominster

Worcester

Northampton

Hereford

Cambridge

Ipswich

Gloucester

Tewkesbury

Oxford

Bristol

Reading

Bath

Devizes

London

Chatham

Bridgwater

Warminster

Canterbury

Portsmouth

```
0          50          100  miles
0      50      100      150  km
```

Map 1. The turnpike road network in 1741

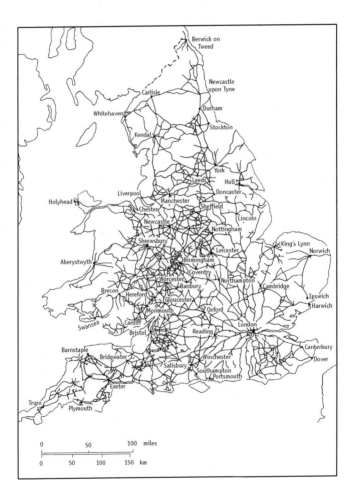

Map 2. The turnpike road network in 1770

for surplus population, or as means of adding to the nation's stock of bullion. The jewels in the imperial crown were the West Indies, with their sugar plantations; the Anglo-Spanish war of 1739, like its predecessors, was seen as a means of breaking into the eldorado of South America, with enticing prospects of gold, silver, and tropical products. Yet in retrospect it is clear that Britain's overseas trade was being recast in the direction of a quite new kind of empire. The dynamic export markets lay increasingly outside Europe, notably in North America. Textiles, the traditional staple, benefited by this redirection, but the growth was still more marked in the newer manufacturing sectors associated particularly with the metal industries, in the production of household commodities, tools, weapons, and all kinds of utensils – in short in the vastly expanding demand for 'Birmingham goods'.

Mercantilist theories were capable of adaptation to accommodate the new trends but it took a time for the process to register clearly with contemporaries. By the 1750s, the full importance of the 13 American colonies was beginning to be appreciated, and the eyes of businessmen and administrators alike were beginning to turn towards competition with France for dominance of the North Atlantic world. The changing emphasis also had important implications in a domestic context. The growth of Georgian London was rapid, and its place as the greatest and most dynamic city in the Western world was already secure. But the fact was that in strictly comparative terms London was less important. A large share of the new trade in the Americas went to new or growing ports in the west, notably Liverpool, Bristol, Glasgow, and for a short but spectacular burst of commercial activity, Whitehaven. The industrial hinterland of these ports, the Severn Valley and West Midlands, the Yorkshire and Lancashire regions, and the west of Scotland, were decisively shifting the industrial base of the country away from the south, east, and west, towards the north and Midlands.

Demographic and Economic Growth

This shift is clearly seen in the demographic trends of the period. After the disasters of the 1720s, population had started growing again, albeit on a very gently rising plateau in the 1730s. The abortive Census proposed in 1750, had it been conducted, would probably have identified a total of about 5.8 million, half a million more than 20 years previously. By 1770 it stood at about 6.4 million, and by 1790 it was approaching 8 million. By nineteenth-century standards this was not a very impressive rate of growth. Nonetheless it represented the crucial turning-point in modern demographic history.

Much the same could be said of industrial and urban growth generally. There was no shortage of important innovations and new enterprises in the late seventeenth and early eighteenth centuries. But between the age of Abraham Darby and the age of Josiah Wedgwood there lay a world of difference. In this respect, the mid-century was again a watershed. The familiar giants of the early industrial revolution, Matthew Boulton and James Watt, Samuel Garbett, Richard Arkwright, Wedgwood himself, made their mark on the national consciousness in the 1760s and 1770s, and it was at the time of the Seven Years War, in the early 1760s, that the full excitement of what was occurring for instance at Birmingham and Manchester began to register.

Urban improvement itself reflected the economic growth and the widespread interest in it. Contemporaries who could remember the reign of Queen Anne and who were to live on into the last quarter of the eighteenth century cited the 1760s and 1770s as a time of extraordinary change and improvement in the material life of the cities, and also to some extent of the smaller towns. The emphasis was on space, hygiene, and order. The expanding towns of Manchester and Glasgow were much admired by visitors for their spacious squares, and neat rows of houses and warehouses. By comparison, the cluttered townscape of the older centres, with its narrow streets and timber-and-thatch housing, seemed outdated and even barbarous. No town with civic self-respect neglected the chance to obtain parliamentary authority for an improvement commission, equipped with extensive powers of rebuilding. Many of the better-preserved towns of today owe their character to this period of urban redevelopment. Perhaps the most spectacular example of imaginative town-planning occurred north of the border; Edinburgh's New Town continues to testify to the vigour of the City fathers in this respect.

The capital of South Britain was not far behind. In a symbolic as well as practical act of modernization, the City of London's medieval gates were demolished in 1761. One of them, Ludgate, had been confidently restored and embellished, with further centuries of service in mind, less than 30 years previously. In nearby Westminster the biggest single project of urban redevelopment was begun at almost the same time in 1762. The Westminster Paving Commissioners and their collaborators in individual parishes were to transform the face of a vast area of the metropolis. Sewers and water-mains were extensively laid or redesigned. Streets and pedestrian walks were cobbled and paved, many for the first time. Squares were cleared, restored, and adorned with a variety of statuary and flora. Houses were systematically numbered; the old signs, colourful, but cumbersome and even dangerous to passers-by, were cleared away. By the 1780s the physical appearance of the capital, with the exception of its slums, was a source of pride to its inhabitants, and of wonder to its visitors, particularly foreigners.

Change was not restricted to cities and towns. Village architecture changed more gradually in most cases, but on the land itself new patterns were emerging. The most celebrated symptoms of the agricultural revolution, the parliamentary enclosure acts, were heavily concentrated in the second half of the eighteenth century. Their economic impact can be exaggerated, for they were statistically less significant than the relatively silent non-parliamentary enclosure which had been proceeding for decades and even centuries; moreover they were principally a feature of the regional belt running south and west from Yorkshire to Gloucestershire. But as pointers to the profitability of agriculture on marginal or convertible land, they are powerful evidence, and in their impact on the landscape they deeply impressed contemporaries. By the time of Adam Smith's *Wealth of Nations*, published in 1776, they suggested a confidence amounting almost to complacency about the continuance of economic growth. Curiously Smith himself did not altogether share this confidence. But Smith was an academic, his work was essentially one of theory rather than practical observation, and much of it had been conceived before the more spectacular developments of the 1760s and 1770s. His countryman John Campbell, whose *Political Survey* (1774) was an unshamed panegyric of Britain's economic progress, is in this respect a surer guide.

Changes in Society

The gathering pace of material growth had an impact on the character of English society. To some extent the results were in line with the trends suggested by commercial diversification and the general advance of capitalism in preceding periods. In terms of social structure, therefore, the principal effect was, so to speak, to stretch the social hierarchy. Because wealth was distributed so unevenly, and because the levels and nature of taxation did so little to redistribute that wealth, real living standards rose much more dramatically in the middle and at the top of the social scale than at the bottom.

This was not altogether new. For example, the development of agriculture in the course of the sixteenth and seventeenth centuries had already noticeably altered the structure of the typical rural community. Enclosure, engrossing, improvement in general were gradually turning village society, characterized by the small property-owner, the freeholder or yeoman beloved of enthusiasts for Old England, into something quite new. Substantial capitalist farmers, frequently tenants of gentry landlords rather than landowners themselves, were coming to dominate an agrarian world in which all below them were increasingly reduced to landless labourers. The process has sometimes been exaggerated, for its actual incidence depended much on local conditions. But it certainly speeded up during the eighteenth century, and, most importantly, had a close counterpart in the development of industrial and urban society. In this sense at least eighteenth-century England was growing into a more polarized society.

Worse, the damaging consequences of polarization were far more apparent. Increased mobility, not to say the large contemporary improvement in literacy and communications generally, made worrying comparisons of rich and poor ever more obvious. The extravagant lifestyle of a ruling elite which seemed to live in a blaze of conspicuous consumption, and also the more modest but cumulatively more influential rise in middle-class standards of living, made the inequalities of a highly commercial, cash-based economy glaringly plain. The *malaise*, if it was a *malaise*, was at its most conspicuous in the capital. Conditions in London, with its relative shortage of well-established social restraints and conventions, its constant tendency to throw the wretchedly poor into close, but profitless, contact with the comfortably bourgeois and even the immensely rich, inevitably gave rise to moral outrage and social criticism of the kind which lives on in Fielding and Hogarth.

How much of the concern reflected an actual worsening of living conditions, it is difficult to judge. Before 1750, very low food prices, combined with the wage stability of a relatively static population, probably increased the real earnings of the poor. The fearful problems arising from the Londoner's thirst for gin – and the less damaging but at the time equally criticized liking of the poorer sort for tea – suggest that at least there was no shortage of disposable income at this time. After the mid-century, however, conditions seem to have deteriorated for many. A return to the older cycle of indifferent and even deficient harvests, together with the episodic slumps and unemployment characteristic of industrial economies, made life at the bottom of the heap a hazardous and harrowing business. Moreover, rapid population growth together with mechanical innovation helped to keep wages relatively low, and ensured that the advantages of industrial expansion were not necessarily shared with the humbler members of an emerging proletariat.

Discontent

The eighteenth century was more sensitive to social problems than it has sometimes seemed, though it had no easy or comprehensive answers. The poor themselves fought back, mainly with traditional weapons in defence of an embattled economic order. Against dearth and high prices, they appealed to ancient laws restricting middlemen and monopolies. Against wage-cutting and the introduction of machinery, they organized combinations to defeat their masters, and clubs to provide an element of social insurance. In extremity, they rebelled and rioted with regularity and enthusiasm.

This was a losing battle, although they were not without their victories. The landed gentry had some sympathy with popular resentment of the activities of moneyed and mercantile entrepreneurs. But the growth of a specialized market for the products of an improving agriculture was as essential to the landlord as to the provisions merchant. Similarly with the antiquated machinery of industrial relations: attempts to enforce the old apprenticeship laws were ineffective against the joint efforts of capitalist manufacturers and unskilled labourers to cheat them. A corporation which succeeded in operating such restrictive practices merely ensured that it did not share in new investment and industry. Associations received even shorter shrift. The friendly clubs, intended purely to provide pensions and sickness benefits, were encouraged by the upper orders. But combinations (or trade unions), even when directed against the more manifest injustices of eighteenth-century employers, such as the use of truck in the west-country clothing industry, were frequently repressed. Where they sometimes succeeded, as in the London tailoring trade, or in the royal dockyards, it was a tribute to the determination of well-established industrial groups. In most of the new industries the employer swept all before him.

The most extreme manifestation of lower-class discontent was in some respects the most tolerated, no doubt because it was seen by paternalistic rulers as a necessary if regrettable safety valve. The measures used to suppress riots were rarely excessive, and punishment was used in an exemplary way on a small number of those involved. Even then, it was often surprisingly light if the provocation seemed extreme and there were no serious implications. Election riots, indeed, were regarded for most of the period as largely unavoidable; in a tumultuous town such as Coventry, with a large electorate and active involvement by those who were not even electors, they were a predictable feature of every election. The recurrent food riots associated with periods of dearth like the mid-1750s and the mid-1760s were also treated as a more or less necessary, if unwelcome, aspect of country life. Within certain limits, there was a wide tolerance in such matters. For instance, the fury of the Spitalfields silk weavers in London in 1765 (when it was believed that the duke of Bedford had worsened their plight by his support for the importation of French silks) brought about something like a full-scale siege of Bedford House. The riots were serious enough to warrant the use of troops, yet even polite London society saw nothing incongruous in treating them as an interesting diversion, worthy of personal inspection from the sidelines.

Persistence, of course, was liable to lead to sterner consequences. Thus, the initial riots against turnpikes in the 1730s were treated with relative good humour, and even a hint of encouragement from some among the propertied classes who resented tolls as much as their lowlier compatriots. But exemplary sentences inevitably followed. Moreover, from the 1760s there were hints of a changing attitude towards popular disturbances. John Wilkes's protracted and controversial campaign in defence of electoral rights and the freedom of the press produced violent demonstrations on the streets. The consequent clashes with authority in the name of 'Wilkes and Liberty' had too many political implications to be viewed with complacency. The anti-papist Gordon riots of 1780, which for the first time produced a real state of terror in London, marked a further important stage in this process. It needed only the French Revolution in the following decade to complete the destruction of the old tolerance and to install the popular riot among the bugbears of the propertied mind.

Poverty and Crime

There were no permanent solutions to the problems engendered by the quantitative growth and qualitative impoverishment of the lowest sort. Poor relief in the eighteenth century continued to be operated on the basis of the Elizabethan Poor Law and the 1662 Act of Settlements. At their worst, these would have put the life of a poor labourer and his family on a par with or perhaps below that of an American slave or a Russian serf. Poor relief might involve the barest minimum of subsistence dependent on ungenerous neighbours, or sojourn in a poor house with consequent exposure to a ruthless master who drew his income from the systematic exploitation of those in his charge. The laws of settlement provided for compulsory residence in the parish of birth for those not occupying a house worth at least £10 per annum, a not insubstantial sum.

In practice, these draconian regulations were less forbidding. Poor relief was a major item in the expenditure of most parishes and by the late eighteenth century was already growing at an alarming rate. It frequently extended to regular outdoor relief and to some extent took account of the rising cost and the rising standard of living. The settlement laws were enforced only to a limited extent. Unhappily their chief victims were women, children, and the old, precisely those who were likely to be a burden on the parish to which they fled. But, even so, restrictions on movement by the second half of the century in reality were slight. The immense labour requirements of industry could hardly have been met if there had been any serious attempt to implement them.

Propertied people felt strongly about the poor in this as in other ages. But they felt still more strongly about crime. For a commercialized society provided ever more temptations, and ever more provocation by way of encouragement to lawlessness. The flashier forms of criminality, such as highway robbery, or the most sociologically interesting, such as offences against the game laws, have traditionally attracted most attention. Those which offended moralists have also intrigued historians. Periodic campaigns for the 'reformation of manners', notably in the first two decades of the century and again in the 1780s, mobilized middle-class volunteers against prostitution, drunkenness, swearing, and gambling. Various kinds of reforming institution were founded, including charity schools, the Foundling Hospital (1739), and the Magdalen Hospital for penitent prostitutes (1758). But the vast majority of crime was one form or another of petty theft, an offence against propertied values which seemed to present a constantly growing threat, particularly in the urban areas. Against this tide of illegality, exaggerated no doubt, but real enough for all that, property in this period had few defences.

Urban crime cried out for effective police forces offering a high chance of detection and conviction (if it did not cry out for kinder cures!). But a police force would have presented many dangers, not least its potential use in terms of political patronage. Moreover the continuing threat represented by any organized force at the command of government was taken very seriously. Few would have seen the point in keeping a standing army to the minimum while permitting a more novel and no less sinister force to spring up in its stead.

In consequence, with few and partial exceptions, for example the efforts of the Fielding brothers in London, the period witnessed no significant improvement in this area. Rather, the authorities were driven back on sheer deterrence, the threat of transportation or death even for relatively insignificant offences. This was the period of the proliferation of capital sentences for minor crimes, against which early nineteenth-century reformers were to fulminate. It seemed the only logical means to stem the flow of crimes against property. Even so it proved self-defeating. For juries would not convict and judges would not condemn in any but the clearest cases. The statistics of conviction are small compared with the actual numbers of offences. Even when the death sentence had been pronounced there was a strong chance of a reprieve at the request of the judge, or at the behest of a highly placed patron. In this way, the processes of justice inevitably sank into the welter of inconsistent policy and political manipulation which marked the period.

The Church

If the poor looked to the State in vain, they looked to the Church with but faint hope. The Church of the eighteenth century has a poor reputation for what would today be called social policy. Entrenched as it was in the patronage structure of the Georgian world, it could hardly be expected to offer a systematic challenge to prevailing attitudes. But it does not altogether deserve its reputation. The sheer volume of eighteenth-century charity is sometimes forgotten. No doubt this is largely because it was overwhelmingly voluntary, and informal. Without the official or State papers which accompany the exercise of charity in a later or even an earlier age it can easily vanish from sight. Yet in terms of the endowment and maintenance of a host of institutions for education, health, and recreation the record is a striking one. It was marked by a frequently patronizing attitude, and motivated in part by an anxiety to keep at bay the social and political threat of the dispossessed. But this is not uncharacteristic of other periods, and the sheer quantity remains surprising. Subscription and association – the central features of this

4. Ladies at leisure. Satirists of the late eighteenth century were struck by the affluence and potential independence of women. John Collet's popular studies (*above and facing*) stress the unladylike nature of some ladies' activities

process – built schools, endowed hospitals, established poor houses, supervised benefit societies. In this the Church, or rather the churches, were heavily involved. Not the least active was a class reviled by later reformers, the dignitaries of the Anglican establishment – its bishops, archdeacons, deans, and canons.

There was, however, a paradox about the Church's position in the eighteenth century. The influence of 'natural' religion in the early part of the century had produced a growing emphasis on works rather than faith.

Christians were those who behaved like Christians, and charity was the most obvious expression of religious devotion. But rational religion, however benevolent, did not offer much spiritual consolation to those who lacked the education or the intellect to be rational. The spiritual energy of all the main churches manifestly wilted under the impact of latitudinarian tendencies. Mainstream dissent, tortured by the theological tensions which arose from the deist challenge to the doctrine of the Trinity, visibly declined as a force in popular life and retreated for the moment at least to its traditional support among the urban middle class. The Church in the rural areas continued its somewhat erratic work, dependent as ever on the residence and personal commitment of a portion of its clergy. In the towns it was all too prone to withdraw, or to appeal, like dissenters, to the polite middle-class congregations who could afford to supplement the poor town livings and to beautify or rebuild churches.

Methodism

It was left to that rebellious daughter of the Church, the Methodist movement, to offer the poor recompense in the next world for their sufferings in this. The many facets and connections of Wesleyan Methodism make it difficult to generalize about its importance. John Wesley himself was an Oxford don of high-church views and unenlightened politics. Yet to many his influence seemed to express something of the Puritan spirit of seventeenth-century religion. His own spiritual journey was tempestuous and marked by what could easily be seen as recklessness and self-will. But the organization and discipline which he bestowed on his followers verged on despotism.

In theological terms, Wesley was an Arminian; but Calvinism exercised a far-reaching effect on the Methodist movement. Indeed Wesley was preceded in the field by Calvinists such as Griffith Jones and Howell Harris in Wales, and George Whitefield in England. To their enemies, all such men seemed dangerous, even seditious characters. Field-preaching could be seen as an open attack on the parish clergy's monopoly of the pulpit; from the vantage point of lay authority, Wesley's readiness to preach his saving message to all ranks and degrees made squires and shires tremble. Yet his political views were positively authoritarian, and he offered no challenge to social order. Through his attitudes and those of his followers ran only one concern: the availability of the evangelist's salvation to all, above all to the poor, to the outcast communities of mining and manufacturing England, neglected by more fashionable divines. It is possible to exaggerate his achievement, for at his death there can hardly have been more than about 70,000–80,000 committed Methodists. Yet the alarm and controversy to which his turbulent life and travels gave rise suggests the extent of his impact on Georgian society. Methodists were accused of an infinity of sins, some of them mutually incompatible. Their preachers were both papists and Puritans, Jacobites and republicans; they ravished wives or influenced them to give up all fleshly pleasures; they coveted other men's goods or denied them the use of worldly possessions. The multiplicity of the charges against Methodism makes it obvious that Wesley touched a tender spot on the contemporary conscience and exposed an embarrassing deficiency in its pattern of beliefs.

Chapter 4
The Making of Middle England

The impression confirmed by the early history of the Methodist movement is very much one of considerable social strains and problems. But it is possible to over-colour the general picture. For one thing it was widely believed at the time that English society avoided the worst of extremes. Foreigners were struck by the flexibility and cohesion of the English social fabric, not by its tensions and rigidities.

A succession of French visitors, from Voltaire to the Abbé Grosley, testified in print to the lack of 'caste' in this country, and especially to the ease with which individuals could move up and down the social ladder. In particular the absence of aristocratic privileges and advantages compared with the Continent earned their applause. Peers might be tried by the House of Lords, but when they went to the gallows they suffered publicly like common criminals. When Lord Ferrers was executed for murdering his servant in 1760 his fate was widely construed as clear evidence that in crime and in death alike the law of England made no distinctions. In a matter of less moment but perhaps no less significance, Grosley was astonished to discover that the tolls on the new turnpikes were paid regardless of rank and without remission for noblemen. Moreover the degradation and dearth which threatened the lives of the urban poor seemed preferable by far to the

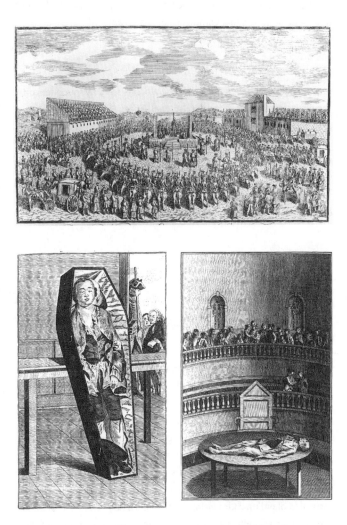

5. The shadow of the gallows. Lord Ferrers, a peer of the realm convicted of murder, suffers the fate of common criminals: public execution at Tyburn and anatomical dissection in the cause of medical science and deterrent example

conditions of French or German peasants. The English labourer (though it must be admitted that commentators usually meant the London labourer) seemed well paid, well fed, and extraordinarily independent and articulate.

Most important of all perhaps was the emphasis laid by foreigners on the flexible definition of the English gentleman. Anyone, it appeared, who chose to dress like a gentleman was treated like one. Middle-class, even lower-class Londoners aped the fashions, manners, and opinions of polite society. This, it seems clear, was the authentic mark of a society in which all social values, distinctions, and customs gave way before the sovereign power of cash. England was the outstanding example in eighteenth-century Europe of a plutocratic society.

Property and Class

The nature of this plutocracy provides a crucial clue to the social stability of the period. On the face of it there was little evidence that the basic structure of property-ownership was changing dramatically. There was no striking surge of bourgeois capital into land, no great expropriation of the landed aristocracy or gentry. The steady assimilation of small professional and business families altered the precise make-up of the landed class without significantly affecting its overall character.

Higher up the scale, the eighteenth century witnessed some strengthening and consolidation of the great landowners. But land was only one form of property and not necessarily the most important. Even at the beginning of the century the primacy of land was diminishing. Estimates of national income at the time of the Glorious Revolution suggest that agriculture contributed nearly a half of the total. But the proportion was changing; by 1780 it was probably down to a third.

In fact, the land itself was merely part of the general commercialization

6. The 'bon ton'. This cartoon of 1777 mocks the enthusiasm of middle-class women for French fashions

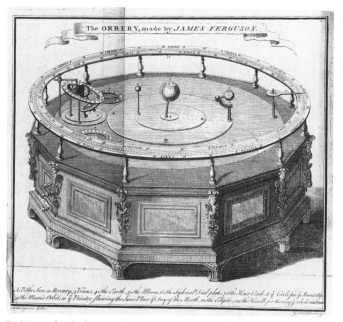

7. Science for the layman. (*Above*): A contemporary print displays the
orrery used by the scientific lecturer and writer James Ferguson to
demonstrate the movements of the planets. Ferguson's lectures fascinated
middle-class audiences in the 1750s, in the provinces and metropolis alike.
The painting of *The Orrery* (*facing*) is by Joseph Wright of Derby, an
enthusiastic interpreter of scientific subjects and one of the Lichfield circle
of amateur scientists

of the English economy; in its exploitation and its improvement, it was
increasingly treated exactly like an investment in stock, in trade, and in
manufacturing. It was noticeable that, whereas temporary agrarian
depressions had little significance for trade, the converse did not hold;
commercial recessions had extremely grave implications for land prices.
In the American War, when overseas trade suffered a disastrous slump,
the effect was instantly seen on property values, with serious political
consequences. If the landed classes had owned the greater part of non-
landed property, the situation would have been very different. But they

plainly did not, whatever their importance in certain sectors such as mining rights and government stocks. Movable goods in the form of industrial capital, personal wealth, and trading balances were overwhelmingly owned by the broad mass of the middle class. On them, primarily, depended the viability and growth of the national economy; and on them too depended the social flexibility and stability which were so much admired by foreigners.

The middle class or 'middling sort' was not, of course, a socially self-conscious or particularly coherent grouping. It remained diverse in point of both wealth and activity. A considerable distance stretched between the city bosses with great mercantile fortunes who ruled the capital, and the small tradesmen or craftsmen who represented the backbone of commercial England – the new 'nation of shopkeepers', a phrase often attributed to Napoleon at the end of the century but in fact used by Adam Smith considerably earlier. Nor was there necessarily much resemblance between the middling countryman, a substantial tenant farmer soon to be dignified perhaps by the title of gentleman farmer, and his urban counterparts, the businessman, doctor, and lawyer, who throve on early industrial society.

Nonetheless, such men had much in common. Frequently self-made and always dependent on aggressive use of their talents, they were genuine 'capitalists' in terms of the investment of their labour and their profits in entrepreneurial activity, whether commercial or professional. Together they owned, controlled, or operated the most dynamic portions of the economy and gradually transformed the common notion of what it was to be an English 'gentleman'. Politically, their supremacy was rarely challenged in towns of any size, and even in many rural parishes they more nearly represented the ruling class than the lordly magnates and oligarchs who seemed so important at Whitehall and Westminster.

Education and Enlightenment

Everywhere the dominant tone of this class, with its pragmatic attitudes and its frankly commercial logic, was discernible. Not least was its influence apparent in education, a matter in which the eighteenth century has acquired a wretched reputation. Inspection of the great institutions of the Tudor and Stuart academic world, the grammar schools and the universities, is not reassuring in this respect.

Grammar schools which continued vigorously to fulfil their function of offering a scholarly education to relatively humble children were few indeed. Most endowments proved inadequate to sustain the expenses or escape the cupidity of those who controlled them. The clergy who taught in them frequently did their best but rarely surmounted the discouraging effects of low salaries and poor support. A few of the old establishments, the Etons, Westminsters, and Winchesters, effectively exploited the developing aristocratic preference for public schooling over private tuition.

The universities in England gave an impression of complacency, particularly by comparison with their Scottish counterparts. North of the border, academic life was characterized by religious strife and even bigotry. But it also displayed signs of immense vigour on which the Scottish Enlightenment prospered. The Scottish contribution to the European achievement of the age in fields as diverse as moral philosophy, political economy, and medical science was substantial. The English universities apparently fell short by this yardstick. Their function was partly to train their clergy, partly to offer a broad education to the genteel and the wealthy. This they performed with more zest than they are generally allowed. The disciplined and innovative instruction offered at a new foundation like Hertford in Oxford, or the genuine progress of mathematical scholarship at Cambridge, by no means confirm the impression given by Thomas Rowlandson's prints or by anti-clerical propaganda. Even so, they plainly did not meet the demands of the middle class.

But the fact was that they were not expected to. In default of the grammar schools and the universities, the characteristically middle-class devices of subscription and fees were bringing into existence a great mass of practical, progressive education designed to fit the sons of the middling sort to staff the professions and the world of business. These schools were often short-lived, and when they passed they left so little behind them that it was easy for censorious Victorians to assume that they had never existed. Even the greatest of the eighteenth-century schools, including dissenting academics like those at Northampton and Warrington, among the best of their kind, withered before very long. But in the meantime they offered exactly the basic, unpretentious education on which the business classes depended. Not that the polite arts and social graces were entirely neglected. Genteel status was as much an aspiration as material wealth. The girls' schools which proliferated in the eighteenth century were well attuned to the social needs of the upwardly mobile. But for boys especially the central virtue of so-called 'modern' schooling was its utility.

The result was emphatically a middle-class culture, with an unmistakably pragmatic tone. If there was an English Enlightenment it was perhaps in this sense, an enlightenment of the practical mind. The fascination of the mid-eighteenth century was not primarily with theological polemics nor with philosophical speculation, but rather with applied technology. The Society of Arts, founded in 1758, was an appropriate expression of this spirit. Perhaps its most controversial project during its early years was a scheme to bring fish from the coast to London by road, thereby breaking the monopoly of the Thames fish dealers, and dramatically lowering the price of a valuable and (it was stressed) a nutritious commodity. It was faintly bizarre, no doubt, but its object was pre-eminently practical.

The Society of Arts was a great national concern, but it was only the most famous of many formal and informal, enduring and ephemeral, clubs and associations which fed on the interest in scientific or pseudo-scientific knowledge. Such interest was at least as enthusiastic in the provinces as in the metropolis. Again, the Lichfield circle associated with Erasmus Darwin and the Lunar Society were only the most celebrated of many amateur groups with earnest attitudes. The stream of literature which they helped to generate also provides a rough index to the growth of popular interest in matters scientific. Even the monthly magazines, designed primarily with a view to entertainment, featured the myriad inventions and speculations of an age deeply committed to the exploration of the physical world.

Recreation

Middle-class work and study required middle-class play and diversions. The eighteenth century will for ever be associated with the amusements of a fashionable oligarchical society, represented most notably in the prime of the first of the great spa towns. Yet Bath would have been a shadow of its Georgian self without its middle-class clientele. The enterprise of the Woods as developers and of 'Beau' Nash as the first master of ceremonies was dependent not merely on the names of the great but also on the money of the middling. For every nobleman reported as taking the waters or attending the Assembly, there had to be a host of those paying for a share in the genteel atmosphere which was created. In this respect, as in so many others, it was the fidelity of the middling sort to the fashions and habits of their social superiors which sustained the commercial viability of leisure and luxury while maintaining the impression of a dominant and patronizing aristocratic elite.

Bath, in any case, was hardly unique. The spas were after all a regional as well as a national phenomenon, offering in the provinces a number of fair imitations of their more celebrated model. When Daniel Defoe toured England in the early 1720s he discovered many spa towns. Tunbridge, he noted with surprise, was a town in which 'company and diversion is the main business of the place'. But Tunbridge had several competitors around the capital: Epsom, Dulwich, and Sydenham Wells all provided attractive resorts for Londoners seeking country air and mineral salts. In the Peak District, already a favourite area for the ancestor of the modern tourist, he found the demands of visitors outstripping the available accommodation at Buxton and Matlock. Buxton, especially, was to grow rapidly in the mid-eighteenth century, though by the 1780s its own rivalry with Tunbridge for second place to Bath was under pressure from a newcomer, Cheltenham.

Spa water, of course, was in limited supply, but there was no shortage of another valuable commodity, sea water. In this as in the case of the spas, the appropriate combination of health and recreation was provided by the co-operation of the medical profession, which hastened to testify to the inestimable benefits of salt water and sea air. Brighton was not developed to any extent until the 1790s. But the development of seaside resorts had begun long before. Dr Russell's *A Dissertation on the Use of Sea Water in the Diseases of the Glands*, published in 1749, was an important influence in this process. Weymouth, which made much of

8. The seaside. (*Above*): An unusual early sketch of the attractions of Blackpool. (*Facing*): An engraving by William Birch after Benjamin West, 1788, showing bathing at Ramsgate; incidentally demonstrated is the use of a bathing machine

the high proportion of minerals in the waters of the English Channel, was already a flourishing resort by 1780. Margate and Ramsgate with easy access from London had established themselves even earlier, and offered more sophisticated and varied arrangements. Scarborough, on the Yorkshire coast was equally advanced.

The medical element in these developments was certainly important. But it is difficult not to see the essential impetus as deriving from more mundane social needs. Between fashionable society with its ritual divisions of the years and its court-oriented timetables, and the despised fairs and holidays of the lower sort, there was a considerable gap, a gap which the new resorts filled with immense success and profit. They were essentially middle-class, urban living transported temporarily to new surroundings, the bourgeois equivalent of the aristocrat's retreat to country-house life. Their underlying basis was the generally felt need for distinctively middle-class recreations. The use of fees or

subscriptions ensured respectable company and a decently moneyed atmosphere.

Particularly for women, in some ways the most obvious beneficiaries of the new affluence, such a flexible, yet protected environment was crucial. Long before the emergence of the resorts, its character had been fully displayed in what Defoe called the 'new fashion'd way of conversing by assemblies'. Assemblies, providing dancing, cards, tea-drinking, and general social mixing, were commonplace by the middle of the century. Even in many market towns they provided an invaluable focus for activities as businesslike as the marriage market, and as casual as country gossip. In the largest cities, spectacular displays of civic pride could be involved; at Norwich the theatre and the assembly hall erected in the 1750s featured striking designs by the local architect, Thomas Ivory. They went up at much the same time as a magnificent new dissenting church, a not inappropriate demonstration of the social link between religion and recreation. Many of those who paid for their admission to the almost daily 'routs' in the Assembly also made their way on Sunday to the chapel.

Cultural Trends

To force all the cultural developments of a complex age into a single pattern might seem incautious. Yet there is little doubt that the dominating tone of the mid-Georgian arts closely corresponded to the needs of a large, wealthy, and pretentious middle class. There was no simple retreat from austere aristocratic classicism to bourgeois romanticism. Rather the classical tradition continued to be reinterpreted as it had been for generations since the Renaissance. But there were signs of a distinctly new and even anti-aristocratic spirit. The triumphs of the Augustan arts had been the triumphs of an elite, intended primarily for the consumption of an elite. Order, structure, and form were the hallmarks of early eighteenth-century art and a sophisticated sense of their classical significance the key to interpreting them. The Horatian satires of a Pope, the Palladian designs of a Burlington, and the still essentially formal landscape gardening beloved of classicists such as William Kent belonged to the same world. But 20 years later few pragmatic products of a middle-class education would have appreciated the linguistic nuances of a satire and fewer still would have understood or identified with the Venetian Renaissance.

By contrast the cultural achievements of the mid-century required neither sophistication nor subtlety. The picturesque gardening publicized by William Shenstone, and still more the vogue for 'natural' landscaping exploited by 'Capability' Brown, represented a major break with the early eighteenth-century passion for classical imitation and allusion. This was also markedly true of the new literary developments. The specifically bourgeois nature of the novel, whether in its picaresque or puritanical form, needs little emphasis. Sometimes, as in Richardson's jaundiced portrayal of rakish aristocrats in *Pamela* and

Clarissa, it was almost painfully prominent. At other times, as in the adventure stories of Smollett and Fielding, it took the form of a moralistic interest in the social life of the lower and middling sort.

In any event these trends came together and produced their most characteristic expression in the triumph of sentiment in the 1760s. Laurence Sterne's *Tristram Shandy*, for example, invaded the palace as well as the parlour, and appealed to the plutocrat as well as the tradesman. But the general enthusiasm for the sentimental movement should not be allowed to obscure its significance as a vehicle of middle-class values and attitudes. Sentiment consummated in fantasy what the wealth of commercial England was bringing nearer in reality, the acquisition of gentility by a consumer society. Sentiment made 'natural' taste, the taste of the virtuous, regardless of upbringing or breeding, the true criterion of gentility; it also boosted the domestic morality of the middle class, with its stress on family life and its devotion to Calvinistic conceptions of virtue, against heroic and hierarchical notions of personal honour.

After George II's death in 1760, the new king and queen were to prove altogether appropriate emblems of such ideals, giving to court society an air which can seem almost Victorian. In this, they faithfully reflected the mores of many of their subjects. Earlier middle classes had merely aped their social betters. Now there was, in theory at least, no need for aping them. Manners in this Brave New World needed no acquiring and a Man of Feeling, like the hero of Mackenzie's influential work of that name, was effectively classless.

Cultural Confidence

If a middle-class culture was sentimental it was also marked by a certain insularity, tempered only by the anxiety of artists themselves to demonstrate their openness to external influences. But activities of intellectual trend-setters in this respect could be somewhat misleading.

Sir Joshua Reynolds, the recognized maestro of English art in the new reign, consciously appealed to Continental models, and saw himself transmitting to a vulgar but expectant public superior traditions of European art. Yet in a way he embodied many of the new trends at home. For Reynolds, like many others who largely owed their living to portraiture, depended as much on a newly moneyed public as on more aristocratic patrons.

In a way too, Reynolds's influence neatly reflected both the national vitality and organized professionalism characteristic of the period. The emergence of the Royal Academy in 1768 saw at one level a representative association comparable to the professional bodies which were beginning to appear on behalf of doctors and lawyers. At another level it brought to a peak a vigorous native art such as Hogarth had heralded but never seen. Not that foreign influences were unimportant in this or in other fields of cultural endeavour. Angelica Kauffmann was the most sought-after decorator of fashionable London, Johann Zoffany one of its most successful portraitists. But neither played the part that resident foreigners had earlier in the century. There was no Verrio dominating the art of grand decoration, no Handel towering over English musicians, no Rysbrack or Roubiliac leading the way in monumental sculpture. Instead, there were the Adams to embellish the Englishman's house, a Burney or Boyce to educate his ear, a Wilton to commemorate his passing.

The new cultural confidence was particularly marked among admirers of English letters. The actor David Garrick pursued a personal campaign on behalf of Shakespeare's plays that culminated in the Shakespeare Jubilee of 1769 at Stratford. But there was matching patriotism among the painters themselves. What had been most striking about Hogarth's self-conscious attempts to create a truly native tradition had been his isolation in this grand enterprise. What was striking about his successors of the English school was the ease with which they felt free to appropriate Continental techniques without a sense of inferiority or dependence. In this respect Joseph Wright of Derby, not the most praised but perhaps the most innovative of mid-century artists, was also thoroughly representative. Appropriately he was a friend of Erasmus Darwin, grandfather of Charles and himself a distinguished physician, scientist, and even poet. Wright was at his best with his semi-educational studies of scientific experiments and discoveries. But he was also the skilled manipulator of light in ways which would not have shamed Caravaggio. Like everyone, Wright went to Italy, but after his major masterpieces, not before; when he returned he seemed to many to have lost rather than gained inspiration.

Politeness and Identity

It was not only in high art that a growing sense of national confidence and coherence, essentially driven by middle-class aspirations, could be viewed. A matter much commented on by visiting foreigners as well as insiders was the growing resemblance between the manners of London and the manners of the country. The dramatist George Colman remarked in 1761 that half a century earlier 'the inhabitants of the distant counties were regarded as a species, almost as different from those of the metropolis, as the natives of the Cape of Good Hope'. Now they were hard to tell apart.

London fashions, London letters, London accents, London diseases spread along the new arterial highways of England and then laterally through the countryside. Edinburgh and Glasgow, Swansea and Dublin, were advance posts in the extension of this process, and when tourism became a major business in the so-called backwood parts of the British Isles from the 1760s and 1770s, further metropolitan conquests were made. No doubt the effects could be exaggerated, though it is striking that much of the contemporary testimony concerned the dress, manner, and morals of the lower class as much as those of the middle. It is possible that at the end of the century the explosive industrial growth of some parts of the country helped create a stronger sense of provincial identity again. But in the middle of the century the perceived emphasis was very much on cultural unification. Dichotomies such as 'court and country' and 'cit and yokel' seemed to be things of the past.

Chapter 5
The Politics of Protest

The social changes which made their mark on mid-Georgian England were profound, extensive, and of the utmost consequence for the future. But their immediate impact on the political structure, at a time when the power of prescription and force of custom were over-riding, is difficult to assess. Superficially there were few changes in the character of politics around the middle of the century. The administrations of Lord North (1770–82) and the younger Pitt (1783–1801) were to provoke comparisons in point of both technique and policy with those of Walpole and Pelham. Of great constitutional changes there were few indeed; the torrent of agitation and reform which threatened the *ancien régime* in the nineteenth century seems in retrospect an unconscionable time arriving.

Yet appearances in this respect were deeply deceptive. The language, the objectives, even the mechanics of politics were all influenced by awareness of a large political nation which lay beyond the immediate world of Whitehall and Westminster. If nothing else the extent and bitterness of the polemical warfare which occurred in newspapers, prints, and pamphlets in the 1750s and 1760s would be adequate testimony to the vitality of public debate and the concern of politicians to engage in it. In this debate, one of the latter seemed to occupy a special place.

William Pitt the Elder

The elder Pitt's reputation is such that, even after two centuries, it is difficult to give him the critical treatment which such an influential figure requires. Before 1754 Pitt's career had been far from an unqualified success. The younger son in a spendthrift and eccentric family, Pitt had joined and eventually married into one of the great Whig houses, that of Temple of Stowe. As a young man he made his political name as a patriot orator of fearsome rhetoric and imprudent vehemence. His anti-Hanoverian outbursts during the War of Austrian Succession acquired widespread publicity and earned him useful popularity, but they rendered him almost permanently *persona non grata* with the king. When, in 1746, the Pelhams were able to offer him office it was on terms which provided profit without prospects. As paymaster-general, Pitt was excluded from the making of high policy and effectively muzzled in parliamentary debate. It seemed yet another example of a patriot's progress, sacrificing principle to promotion.

But Pitt's fortunes were dramatically changed by the events of the mid-1750s. The sudden death of Henry Pelham in 1754 seemed even at the time a watershed, indicated not least by the king's own observation on its significance: 'Now I shall have no more peace.' Pelham's successor was his brother, Newcastle, a shrewd, experienced minister, and by no means the ridiculous mediocrity portrayed by legend. But from the Lords he found it difficult to exercise the controlling influence either of his brother or of Walpole. Pitt's principal rival in the Commons, Henry Fox, lacked the political courage or weight to replace Pelham. The 'old corps' of Whigs, the dominant force in Parliament since the Hanoverian accession, was almost without leadership. Their Tory opponents, by now increasingly restive under continuing proscription and no longer disposed to think seriously of a king over the water, also sought inspiration. Could not Pitt provide what both needed?

That he was able to do so owed much to circumstance, and in particular to the international situation. The War of Austrian Succession had identified major areas of conflict for the future without beginning to settle them. The principal focus overseas was no longer the fate of the Spanish empire, but the world-wide conflict threatening between Britain and France, in a mercantilist age the most successful mercantilist powers. In North America, the French sought to forge a chain from Quebec to Louisiana, cutting off the English colonies. In the West Indies there was constant bickering over disputed sugar islands, as there was in West Africa over the trade in slaves and gum. In India the factiousness and feebleness of native princes combined with the rapacity of the French and English East India Companies to create a volatile situation. Everything pointed to a desperate and conclusive war for empire.

Pitt and the Seven Years War

When it came it began disastrously both for England and for Pitt's political rivals. In 1755–6, naval operations were ineffectual. The loss of Minorca in the Mediterranean, and the cynicism with which the scapegoat Admiral Byng was sacrificed, left the old Whig regime discredited. This was the making of Pitt, and perhaps of the First British Empire.

The ensuing years have taken their place in history as a period of exceptional importance. The successes of the Seven Years War, which decisively defeated France in North America and India, and turned back the Bourbon threat elsewhere, represented a high point of imperial achievement and made Pitt the most gloriously successful war minister in British history. Moreover, his triumph in trouncing the 'old corps' politicians seemed to suggest a new kind of politician and a new kind of politics, neatly encapsulated in Dr Johnson's contrast between Walpole as a 'minister given by the king to the people', and Pitt as a 'minister given by the people to the king'. Yet Pitt made his way to power more by shrewd political judgement and sheer luck than by public acclaim.

His supposedly popular support was engineered by his friends in the City of London and by his new-found Tory associates in the provinces. His first essay in power, the Pitt–Devonshire ministry of 1756–7, was weak and short-lived; his second, the coalition of 1757, was much more successful, thanks partly to a deal with Newcastle, partly to the support of the Prince of Wales, the future George III. This combination of the reversionary interest and the 'old corps' was as cynical an exercise in political manoeuvre as anything conceived by Pitt's predecessors and opponents; it corresponded closely with what Walpole had done in 1720 when he and Prince George (the later George II) had bullied and wheedled their way back to court.

Nor did the war quite present the unblemished record which Pitt's admirers were to make of it. The fundamental strategy which Pitt pursued was completely at variance with the patriot programme which he had previously espoused. His commitment to an expensive alliance with Prussia and his generous deployment of British resources in both money and men to maintain an army in Germany followed naturally from the diplomatic strategy of Pelham and Newcastle. Pitt's own most characteristic contribution to the war, his use of combined operations against the coast of France, designed to divert French attention from the war in Germany, was a desperate attempt to prove his patriot credentials to his friends the Tories, already increasingly dismayed by his 'Hanoverian' policies. In military terms, they were wasteful and largely ineffective.

When victory eventually came, it owed much to forces over which Pitt had little control. In general, the French paid heavily for their failure to build up resources for naval and colonial warfare. In India, the advantage enjoyed by the British East India Company was marginal but it was decisive, particularly when the talents of Robert Clive were thrown into the balance. Pitt's description of Clive as a 'heaven-born' general was a rhetorical admission that he could not claim the credit for Clive's appointment himself.

Even James Wolfe, whose heroic assault on Quebec captured the national imagination, was only the last of a number of commanders whose activities in North America by no means achieved uniform success. But victory solves all problems in war, at least until a peace has to be negotiated. Before the *annus mirabilis* of 1759, when the tide turned both in the West Indies and in North America, Pitt's coalition with Newcastle was precariously balanced on the brink of disintegration. Pitt's Tory supporters constantly talked of deserting a minister whose policies filled them with alarm, while his ally Newcastle repeatedly threatened to ditch a colleague who spent money like water in pursuit of costly defeats. In 1759 these difficulties dissolved.

Pitt did not fully deserve the credit for the fortunes of the Seven Years War, but there were two important respects in which his historical reputation seems justified. For if Pitt's popular credentials have been exaggerated, his role in changing the character of eighteenth-century politics was nonetheless an important one. In the mid-1750s the mould was plainly cracking. The proscription of Toryism, and the ability of the Whig families to keep the control of patronage within a narrow circle, had a very short future. Pitt offered at least the hope of a break with the old politics, especially in the metropolis where his connections went deep into a genuinely popular electorate. Similarly, as a war leader he did provide one crucial quality which no rival possessed at this time, without which the war could not have been continued, let alone brought to a triumphant conclusion. Political courage, and with it a confidence which was difficult to distinguish from unthinking arrogance, gave other more competent and cautious men the moral base on which to fight and win a brilliant war. Pitt's faith in his own leadership provided a key component in the direction of the war at the very moment when the leaders of the old Whig gang, Newcastle and Fox, had manifestly lost their nerve. If political laurels go in the last analysis to those prepared to risk everything, then in this sense at least Pitt deserved them.

The Return of the Tories

Whatever the nature of Pitt's achievement, his controversial activities formed a fitting prologue to the drama which was shortly to follow. The transformed character of politics in the 1760s will be for ever associated with the new king George III and with one of his most turbulent subjects, John Wilkes. So far as the king was concerned these years were to prove traumatic in the extreme. Yet much of what George III did was the logical culmination of trends in his grandfather's reign. This was particularly true of his supposedly revolutionary determination to abolish the old party distinctions. The validity of such distinctions had already been diminished by the success of Frederick Prince of Wales and Pitt in enlisting the aid of the Tories. The difference in 1760 was one of tone rather than substance, with reluctant and grudging toleration being replaced by unavowed pride in the accessibility of the new regime to the old Tories. At court, they were welcomed back with open arms and with a judicious distribution of offices, honours, and peerages. In the counties, they returned, where they had not returned during the preceding decade, to the commissions of the peace; in the midland shires the commissions once again resembled a roll call of the country gentry, many of them of old Tory and even old royalist stock.

One redoubtable Tory was granted a special place in the sun. Dr Johnson, the literary giant of the age, basked in the political approval of the new regime, signalized with a pension from Lord Bute in 1762. His new acceptability was not without irony. In the 1730s Johnson had written a bitter patriot attack on the pro-Spanish policy of Walpole in relation to the Caribbean, and British claims there. Now, under the new king, he was to pen an equally powerful and more compelling piece in defence of George III's supposed appeasement of Spain over the British claim to the Falkland Islands, which he described as 'a bleak and gloomy solitude, an island thrown aside from human use, stormy in winter, and barren in summer'. This was not the end of the Falkland Islands as an issue in the history of British foreign policy.

What Johnson's progress as an individual signified was still more strikingly endorsed institutionally in the history of Oxford University. For 46 years the home and shrine of sentimental Jacobitism had suffered in the political wilderness, as successive generations of Whig churchmen monopolized the places of honour and profit. The ecclesiastical masters of early Hanoverian England had generally been trained either at Cambridge or at the tiny minority of Whig colleges at Oxford. In the new reign, there was no doubt which university made its emotional home-coming. Oddly enough, Oxford had contributed more than one prime minister even to early Hanoverian government. But Pelham had made little attempt to prevent his brother's direction of ecclesiastical patronage to Cambridge, and Pitt had at one time stooped to making capital of his own university's Jacobite associations. Under George III, Oxford was to have in Lord North a prime minister who was also its chancellor, and one who fittingly represented the old Tory families of the cavalier counties.

If the return to court of the Tories was unsurprising, George III's other new measures seem hardly less so. The reign began in a haze of good intentions and lofty aspirations. Any notion that a new 'patriot king' might seek to strengthen the royal prerogative was quickly crushed. The Demise of the Crown Act, which stipulated that judges would not as in the past resign their offices at the death of the sovereign, removed any suspicion that kings might use their legal rights to sweep away the Whig judicial establishment. At the same time, the Civil List Act provided for a strictly controlled royal allowance of £800,000 per annum; this was the same as that granted to George II, but there was the important additional provision that any surplus produced by the civil list duties was for the future directed to the Exchequer, not to the Crown. With inflation, this stipulation was seriously to impede the Crown's capacity to cope with the rising tide of court expenses and ironically proved to be a most damaging concession by the king in the name of patriotic propriety. This was the true legacy of the Leicester House party under Frederick Prince of Wales – not a fanciful scheme for the creation of a new benevolent despotism, but further limitation of the Crown's prerogative.

Peace

These, however, were minor matters compared with the most important of the new regime's priorities – peace. The old ministers, Pitt and Newcastle, both resigned from office, the former in 1761 because George III and Bute declined to extend the war to Spain at his insistence, the latter specifically in protest against the peace terms the next year. But most of the arguments which they deployed carry little weight in retrospect. Peace could not be secured without restoring to the Bourbons a proportion of the gains made during the war. The return of the principal French West Indian Islands and the preservation of French fishing rights in Canadian waters were not excessive concessions, nor would Pitt and Newcastle, in the diplomatic circumstances of 1762, have been able to make less without continuing the war to the bitter end.

Moreover the immense successes of recent years had been gained at a fearful financial cost, which by 1761 was provoking widespread alarm. The case against further prosecution of the war, put repeatedly in newspapers and pamphlets and led by Israel Mauduit's *Considerations on the German War*, was a strong one. War *à outrance* would end in bankruptcy; moreover its object – continued support of Frederick the Great and the acquisition of some additional colonial possessions – seemed of doubtful value. It is possible that George III and Bute, moved in part by the reflection that the war, for all its glory, was not their war, and influenced also by the need to make a quick peace, surrendered rather more than they needed to, particularly in the terms they made with Spain. But in essentials their peace was a prudent, defensible measure and was overwhelmingly approved by parliamentary and public opinion.

Personal Enmities

Why, in these circumstances, did the new reign prove so controversial? Mainly, perhaps, it was because the new men brought to their otherwise innocuous activities a degree of personal animosity towards the old regime which was bound to cause difficulties. The chosen instrument of George III's reforms was his former tutor, Lord Bute, a Scottish peer of intellectual bent whose experience and skills were slight. Most of the instruction with which he had prepared the young king for his task was

9. Royalty refulgent. (*Above*): Zoffany's painting of the royal family captures both the confident regality of the new king, George III, and the somewhat theatrical neo-classicism of the 1760s. The new king was not afraid to challenge comparison with his Stuart forebears, as the Van Dyck costumes show; the Jacobite threat was dead and the appeal of Charles I could safely be used to glorify the Hanoverian line. (*Overleaf*): Lord Bute's role as royal favourite brought him exceptional vilification in the press. This cartoon of 1767 employs a commonplace image for eighteenth-century prime ministers – 'The Colossus' – but also specifically attributes Bute's success to fraud (his use of royal influence) and lust (his supposed seduction of the king's mother, the princess dowager of Wales)

more naive than knavish. There was no great conspiracy against liberty and the constitution, nor any determination to introduce a new authoritarian system. But there was undoubtedly on the part of the new king and his minister a deep-seated resentment of the men who had monopolized power under George II and a readiness if not a determination to dispense with, even to humiliate, them. For 'black-hearted' Pitt, who was seen as betraying the prince's court in 1757, there was outright hatred, and it is difficult to see how Pitt and Bute could have co-operated in the new circumstances. But Pitt was a megalomaniac with whom only a saint could have co-operated for long.

The great Whig families were another matter. Their rank, weight, and inherited importance would make them dangerous enemies. No doubt they treated the new king with a measure of condescension. Families such as the Cavendishes were apt to regard themselves as kingmakers, for whom the electors of Hanover were at most *primi inter pares*. Newcastle, after a lifetime in office, might be forgiven for expecting to have his advice taken seriously by a donnish, ineffectual Scottish peer who was chiefly known for the shapeliness of his legs and his patronage of botanists. There were, in short, good reasons for proceeding cautiously, and above all reasons for ensuring as smooth a transition as possible between the new and the old politics.

This was by no means out of the question. The 'old corps' Whigs knew well that the substance of Bute's demands must be granted. Most of them, in the absence of a charismatic leader of their own, were content to labour on under new management. A typical figure was Lord North, himself a cousin of the duke of Newcastle, a future prime minister and in the new reign a passive adherent of George III's court. Even the senior men, who saw themselves as victims of the new order, were reluctant to declare war on it. Lord Hardwicke, the doyen of Whig lawyers and one of the pillars of the Pelhamite system, sought only dignified provision for his friends and a continuing supply of places at court for his family.

Given this background, it was maladroit of Bute and George II to drive out Newcastle and his friends. When they did so, ostensibly over the peace terms in the spring of 1762, they created one of the most enduring enmities in modern British politics.

Perhaps the alienation of the old political establishment would have been a price worth paying if the new plans had worked out. But Bute himself, having beset his young charge with powerful enemies, chose to resign from office after only a year, with the lordly intention of directing affairs from the backbenches, or rather (as it was inevitably seen) from the backstairs. And so to the folly of antagonizing the old Whig families was added that of providing them with a legend of intrigue and influence with which to sustain and inspire their opposition. This opposition and the equivocal conduct of Bute set the pattern for 20 years or more of politics.

In the short run, the 1760s featured a nightmarish cycle of ministerial instability, as George III sought a minister who was both congenial in the closet and capable of presiding in Parliament. In the process, the Whigs themselves under Lord Rockingham, Pitt, and the duke of Grafton were tried and found wanting, until in 1770 Lord North emerged as a figure capable of wearing the mantle of Walpole and Pelham. Running through these years of tortuous, factious politics there was always the *damnosa hereditas* of Bute's inconsequential yet damaging flirtation with power, the suspicion of the Whig families, and the myth of a continuing, improper, secret influence. When Edmund Burke produced his comprehensive and classic analysis of the politics of the period, *Thoughts on the Cause of the Present Discontents* (1770), it was this influence which gave him the basis for a systematic onslaught on the new court and its system. The *Thoughts* were to pass into history as the authorized version of the Whig party, and for many later generations the standard account of the misdeeds of George III.

The Wilkesite Movement

There was other inflammable material at hand in the 1760s. The war was succeeded by a serious economic slump which clearly demonstrated the uneven distribution of economic rewards in the age of enterprise. The period was marked by a series of violent industrial disputes which created unrest in urban centres such as Manchester and Newcastle, and threatened to spill over into political agitation. Even in the countryside these were years of bad harvests, rising prices, and serious dearth.

In this atmosphere the activities of John Wilkes found ample support.

Wilkes's historical reputation as an amiable rogue has, to some extent, obscured his political shrewdness and inventiveness. Circumstances and opportunism were the making of Wilkes. The grievances which he took up would have made little impact 10 years earlier. The general warrants, which permitted arbitrary arrest for political offences, and which caused so much controversy when Wilkes's journalistic activities provoked George III's ministers to deploy them, had been a familiar feature of Hanoverian government. They were used, for example, by both Pitt and Newcastle in their time. But then they had been justified by reference to the Jacobite threat, and they had been used against proscribed Tories rather than vociferous Whigs.

Similarly when, in 1768, Wilkes stood for the county of Middlesex and found himself barred from his seat in the Commons there were tolerable precedents and adequate legal arguments for his exclusion. But the Middlesex election involved a popular county intimately connected with the feverish politics of the capital; the Middlesex electors could not be treated as if they were a handful of voters in a rotten borough. Three years later, when Wilkes and his friends attacked the right of the House of Commons to prevent the public reporting of its debates, they were attacking an old and jealously guarded privilege of the legislature. But the defence of that privilege proved hopelessly impracticable in the new climate.

The Wilkesite radicals were typically small businessmen, craftsmen, and artisans. They represented the 'middling and inferior sort' at its most concentrated, its most articulate, and its most volatile. When they took their grievance to the country they found support not only among provincial gentlemen worried by the threat to electoral rights but also among their own counterparts in towns up and down the country. The middle class, the crucial element in their campaign, had no unified politics, and protest was not normally their preferred political role. But their part in the Wilkesite movement unmistakably signalled their importance in the politics of George III's reign.

Yet this importance was only in part of their own making. The rules by which the political game had been played under the early Hanoverians no longer applied, whatever precedents they offered; for the men who had found them advantageous now found it convenient to abandon them. The old Whigs, by their readiness to use any weapon of revenge against George III, did much to legitimize the new spirit of popular opposition to the court. Without this collaboration from highly respectable elements in the ruling class, the popular convulsions associated with Wilkes would have been of less consequence.

True Britons

Nothing that occurred in the 1760s threatened George III's hold on his kingdoms. Yet awkward questions were raised about the public emotions that underpinned it. The mid-century wars had generated much patriotic rhetoric in praise of Britishness. But the Britannia that ruled the waves was in England likely to be thought of as English rather than British. The Union of 1707 had divided the island into North and South Britain. This terminology made no appeal south of the border.

George III boasted publicly of glorying 'in the name of Briton'. There were those who would have preferred him to glory in the name of Englishman. As it became clear that Bute and a phalanx of his countrymen were among the principal beneficiaries of the new patriotism, resentment grew. Immigrant Scots were prominent in the business and professional life of London. The numerous doctors turned out by Scottish universities were well equipped to meet the medical needs of a burgeoning class with money to spend on health. But the process of social and ethnic integration was not painless. The Wilkesites adroitly exploited populist anti-Scottishness. The seditious journal with which Wilkes himself began his tempestuous radical career was entitled *The North Briton*. Unfavourable national stereotypes of the Scots retained their currency for much of the late eighteenth century. Not until another period of prolonged warfare during the Revolutionary and

Napoleonic era did the rhetoric of Britishness soften if not obliterate these.

Anti-Irish sentiment was also commonplace but operated at the level of casual abuse and prejudice rather than political agitation. Even so, the 1760s had a destabilizing effect on Irish politics itself. In Dublin as in London the object was to displace the men and families that had long monopolized power. But here too the unintended effect was to unleash many unruly elements. As a result there arose some troublesome demands, for more parliamentary control of Irish affairs, for greater freedom of trade, and (not always from the same voices) for a measure of Roman Catholic emancipation. Violent peasant unrest and the stirrings of a new Irish nationalism, ambivalent in its religious undertones but strident in its dislike of government from London, set the scene for what was to prove a crisis in Anglo-Irish affairs. The impetus for that crisis came not, however, from within the British Isles but from more distant dependencies of the crown.

Chapter 6
Rebellion and Reform

The early years of the new reign have always attracted attention for their colourful politics. Yet in some ways the most striking changes of the period concerned Britain's role overseas, especially the new awareness of empire which inevitably succeeded the Seven Years War.

West and East

The effective hegemony of North America was especially entrancing. Imperial civil servants and ministers enjoyed a brief period of uninhibited inventiveness in the early 1760s as they planned a new and rosy future for the transatlantic colonies. Quebec was to provide a veritable cornucopia of fish and fur. The American colonies, reinforced by settlement in Canada and the Floridas, would form a vast, loyal market for British manufactures, a continuing source of essential raw materials, and even (enticing prospect for a debt-ridden mother country) a new source of revenue for the Treasury. The West Indies, firmly entrenched in a more effectively policed mercantilist system, would maximize the benefits of a flourishing slave trade, provide a steady flow of tropical products, and form a valuable base for commercial incursions into the Spanish Empire.

In the East still more speculative and still more exciting prospects appeared. After Clive's victory at Plassey in 1757 Britain had emerged as

10. The Younger Pitt: for and against. The favourable portrayal (*above*) is
Gainsborough's, the unfavourable (*overleaf*) Gillray's. Comparison of the
latter with the cartoons on pages 24–5 demonstrates how far the art of
political caricature had advanced since the Walpole era

the dominant European power on the subcontinent. There was, technically, no territorial presence in the East Indies, but in reality from this time the British East India Company was inextricably involved in effective colonization. In this respect 1765, when Clive formally accepted the diwani (land revenues) of Bengal on behalf of the company and thereby committed it to direct political control rather than mere commercial activity, was a landmark as important as Plassey itself, even if it followed logically from it.

These events transformed the British perception of India. The exotic

11. Father and son. The contrast between George III and his son was even more striking than that between other Hanoverian fathers and sons. The king and his wife (*above*) provided for Gillray a model of sober domesticity; here they are shown on their way to their beloved Windsor, much in the manner of any other farmer and his wife returning from market. Prince George (*overleaf*), on the other hand, identified himself with the morally dissolute and politically subversive; he is shown the morning after his ill-concealed and unauthorized marriage to Mrs Fitzherbert in 1785

character of the new possessions and the fact that they brought to light a previously unappreciated culture made the impact of the new empire particularly powerful. This impact was early expressed by Francis Hayman's massive portrayal of Clive receiving the submission of native princes, erected at that pantheon of genteel amusements, Ranelagh, in 1765. Imports of Asian curiosities soared and for the first time something like an informed and genuine interest in Indian society began to take shape.

Other aspects of the new acquisitions in the East were less refined and less affecting. In the general election of 1768, a noticeable feature of press reporting was the appearance in a number of constituencies of men who had returned from service in the East India Company and were

The MORNING after MARRIAGE ___ or ___ A scene on the Continent.

using their allegedly ill-gotten wealth to buy their way into Parliament. The 'nabobs' had arrived. Their influence was invariably exaggerated, as were their misdeeds and villainies. Moreover, in principle they were no different from the West India planters, the 'Turkey merchants', the 'moneyed men', and others whose unconventional profits had incurred the enmity of older, less 'diversified' families. But their appearance was inevitably a matter of intense curiosity and eventually concern.

Clive himself was the embodiment of the rapacious 'nabob'; the ruthlessness and unashamedness with which he had acquired personal riches while in the service of the company seemed all too representative of an entire class of men who saw empire as the means to a fast, and even felonious fortune. Nor, it seemed, were temptations restricted to India. The furious speculation in East India stock which followed the grant of the *diwani*, the consequent recurrent crises in the company's financial affairs, and not least the government's growing interest in its activities all brought the complex and frequently corrupt character of East India politics into an unwelcome and glaring light.

The American War

America had no nabobs, but the economic and political problems caused by the preservation and extension of the American empire were greater even than the results of Eastern expansion, and their ramifications still wider. British ministers saw all too clearly the potential value of their transatlantic subjects, but they did not appreciate the extent to which the 13 colonies had developed an independent attitude when it came to intervention from London. Nor did they grasp the capacity of a distant, wealthy, and resourceful population of some two and a half million to obstruct and resist imperial power. The result was a decade of cyclical crisis in Anglo-American relations, beginning with the Stamp Act, which raised the American cry of 'no taxation without representation' in 1765, and finally culminating in rebellion and war in 1775.

It is not easy to identify what, in the last analysis, was at issue from the British standpoint, even at two centuries' distance. By 1775 most of the aims of the post-war ministers had been explicitly or tacitly abandoned. Not even the most optimistic can have thought by 1775 that America was going to prove what Lord Rockingham called a 'revenue mine'. Quelling the colonies by force was bound to be as expensive as its ultimate consequences were bound to be unpredictable. European enemies would plainly see the War of Independence as an opportunity to redress that balance which had tilted so much to their disadvantage in the Seven Years War. Moreover there were those who challenged the entire basis of the war as a logical conclusion from mercantilist principles. Adam Smith's *Wealth of Nations*, published in the same year as the Declaration of Independence (and incidentally at the same time as the first volume of Edward Gibbon's pessimistic survey of the Roman Empire), systematically demolished the economic case for empire.

Yet with a few exceptions, notably the radical politicians of the metropolis and some of the religious dissenters, Englishmen strongly supported the war against America. Its central principle, the defence of unlimited parliamentary sovereignty, was naturally important in this, the great age of that principle. William Blackstone's celebrated *Commentaries on the Laws of England*, published in 1765, had announced with uncompromising clarity the unbounded legal authority of the Crown-in-Parliament; the conflict with America was its clearest possible expression. Moreover, the economic arguments which seem so attractive in retrospect made little impression when they were first put. For most Englishmen the only viable concept of empire was the old mercantilist one. Colonies which declined to accept the full extent of parliamentary supremacy were not merely worthless, they were positively dangerous. Against this belief that an empire out of control was worse than no empire at all, more imaginative minds made little progress.

Here, if ever, there was a clash of chronology and culture. Americans at heart were defending the rights of seventeenth-century Englishmen. For them, resistance to the stamp tax was on a par with John Hampden's struggle against Ship Money; a sovereignty which over-rode provincial assemblies and local rights was unthinkable. The English, on the other hand, were deploying an eighteenth-century weapon, parliamentary supremacy, in support of what was one of the eighteenth century's most cherished doctrines, the indivisible and unlimited authority of metropolitan power in a mercantilist system. Only force would decide the outcome.

In due course, the outcome was determined in favour of the new United States. In the interim the war proved a disaster for Britain – worse by far than anything since the Second Dutch War of 1665–7. It grew from being a colonial insurgency to an all-out war against the Bourbon monarchies, and eventually involved hostilities with the Dutch and a state of 'armed neutrality' with other powers. At the peace negotiations of 1782–3 a certain amount was saved from the wreckage. Although the 13 colonies were lost irretrievably, a brilliant naval victory at 'the Saints' by Admiral Rodney in 1782 preserved the British West Indies and above all saved George III the embarrassment of surrendering what Oliver Cromwell had gained over a century before, the much-prized jewel of Jamaica. In the Mediterranean, Spain's attempt at the reconquest of Gibraltar was foiled. In India, Warren Hastings's redoubtable defence of Clive's acquisitions staved off both French *revanche* and princely rebellion.

Closer to home still more desperate efforts had to be made to retain control of Ireland. The American War on the one hand put intense economic and military pressure on Ireland and on the other provided invaluable leverage for Irish patriots bent on loosening British dominion. In 1780 North in effect gave Irish traders equal rights within the imperial economy. In 1782 Rockingham formally recognized the legislative independence of Ireland. In the circumstances keeping Ireland within the empire could be pictured as something of a triumph. Contemporaries found the independence of America a bitter pill to swallow, but most of the empire outside the 13 colonies remained intact, and at least the utter humiliation feared in the darkest days of the war was averted.

The Association Movement

Almost more important than the overseas consequences of the American War were the domestic implications. The economic problems caused to a nascent industrial society by a world war and the accompanying embargoes on trade were immense. In the ensuing recession both the stock market and land values plunged to alarmingly low levels, unseen in many years. Unprecedentedly high taxes and the rapid growth of the National Debt reinforced the financial crisis and created serious economic problems. Fundamental questions were raised about government, Parliament, and the political system generally. In the ensuing chaos, relatively conservative forces, not least the country gentry, were swept into what looked like an open attack on the constitution, with the Association movement of 1779–80. The Associations had widespread support in the counties, the capital, and provincial cities, and in their demands for reform went further than all but the wilder radicals of the Wilkesite movement. Christopher Wyvill, the Yorkshire cleriygman and country gentleman who came close to exercising national leadership of the movement, was hardly himself such a radical. Yet his demands for the elimination of rotten boroughs, the extension of the franchise, and the introduction of the secret ballot had a futuristic ring. Moreover, there was about the Associations a hint, or in the mouths of metropolitan agitators such as John Jebb and Major Cartwright a definite suggestion, that Parliament, if it resisted reform, should be superseded by the delegates of the counties.

Contemporary fears of this new phenomenon were overly colourful. Yet in retrospect it is difficult not to be struck by the vigour and extent of the Association movement. It arguably brought reform nearer than at any time in the ensuing 50 years, and at its height in 1780 it achieved an extraordinary degree of national consensus. At this point even the House of Commons, notwithstanding the weight of vested interests in and out of government, passed a resolution declaring that the 'influence of the crown has increased, is increasing and ought to be diminished'. This was the signal for almost five years of intense political controversy and sustained ideological conflict.

Why, then, did the Association movement fail to fulfil its promise? When Lord North gave way to a brief period of Whig rule in 1782 Burke and his colleagues pushed through Parliament a handful of reforms abolishing some of the more notorious sinecure places and providing for a closer scrutiny of Crown finances. But parliamentary reform proved elusive. Even when the younger Pitt was granted supreme power in 1783 and reform was duly proposed from the Treasury bench with the prime

12. Civilizing mission. Despite the success of the Union, Scots endured much hostility in England. This comment on the unfamiliarity of a Scotsman with the conveniences of London life was originally published at the time of the Forty-Five but reproduced on subsequent occasions

minister's authority, there was nothing like a parliamentary majority for it.

In large measure this had to do with the circumstances in which the Association movement was born. Enthusiasm for root-and-branch reform was limited, and generally confined to the articulate and the urban. It sometimes made a disproportionately loud noise but real support even among the urban bourgeoisie was restricted. Eighteenth-century Parliaments, whatever their electoral inadequacies, were highly sensitive to the demands of small and middling property-owners. Much legislation was directed to their commercial and industrial interests. Still more empowered them in their localities, on all kinds of statutory bodies, from turnpike and canal trusts to improvement commissions and poor law corporations. To those who benefited, the case for parliamentary reform looked thin.

Association sprang from a national crisis in which any systematic critique of the existing politics would have proved attractive. The outcry of the reformers against the waste and inefficiency of the court system seemed particularly appropriate. The same phenomenon was to appear for the same reason 30 years later when the immense expenditure of the Napoleonic Wars and the economic crisis associated with it produced similar protests. But these conditions were short-lived and most of the interest in reform died with them. By the mid-1780s there was a growing sense of commercial revival and financial recovery, not least due to the impact of the younger Pitt's policies. Prosperity removed the stimulus to reform more effectively than any argument could.

An additional consideration was the wide and growing concern at the measures of the extremists. The lunatic fringe of the reform movement seemed to be challenging not merely the corrupt politics of the court, but the constitutional framework which supported it, and even the propertied order itself. What was to become the 'Rights of Man' school was already visible in the writings of the early reform movement. Men such as Richard Price and Joseph Priestley were, by the standards of a later age, moderate enough. But they were challenging some of the most entrenched attitudes and commonplace ideas of their day and it needed very little to force apart their fragile alliance with backwoods gentry and provincial business men.

13. Civilizing mission. Exploration of the South Pacific aroused widespread public interest and gave much scope for the cult of the noble savage, tinged with a certain prurience, as in these illustrations to G. Keate's *Account of the Pellew Islands*, 1788. Lee Boo (*above*) was exhibited in England as a curiosity and also treated as a living educational experiment; before the experiment had lasted six months he died of smallpox. Ludee (*overleaf*) remained in her island paradise, but as an example of native beauty she was deemed no less instructive

Riot and Reaction

In this context the Gordon Riots proved particularly damaging. There was no direct connection between the reformers and the Gordon rioters, who in the spring of 1780 held London at their mercy for nearly a week and engaged in an orgy of murder and destruction. Their cause was unashamed religious prejudice, their aim to repeal the liberal measure of relief for Roman Catholics which had been passed with the support of both government and opposition in 1778. As with the Jew Bill

in 1753–4, it was clear that the legislature could easily get out of step with popular feeling. The leader of the anti-papists, Lord George Gordon, called his movement the Protestant Association, and it was easy enough for frightened men of property to make a connection between the rioters and the political activities of more respectable Associators. The conservative reaction so marked in England during the following years could perhaps be traced back to this episode.

The early 1780s were not only turbulent in the extra-parliamentary sense; they also provided the same spectacle of political instability as the 1760s. This, too, was an element in the failure of reform. Before 1782 reformers in Parliament had congregated loosely around the two main Whig groups, Lord Rockingham's party and those who followed Lord Shelburne. The two wings of recognized Whiggism represented distinct traditions going back to Newcastle and the old Whig clans in the case of Rockingham, and to the elder Pitt in that of Shelburne. The most promising talent in each was also a familiar name. Charles James Fox, one of Rockingham's most radical supporters and also his most popular, was the son of that Henry Fox who had been a rival to the elder Pitt, and in the new reign briefly a tool of Lord Bute. Among Shelburne's associates was the younger Pitt – in Burke's phrase, not 'a chip off the old block' but 'the block itself'. Both were authentic reformers, both seemed to offer a fresh approach to a jaded, yet optimistic age, both held out the hope of leadership against the discredited politics of the men who had mismanaged the American War.

Unfortunately, if perhaps inevitably, they turned out to be rivals rather than allies, and in the complex, bitter politics which followed Lord North's resignation in 1782, their enmity proved crucially important. The initiative was taken by Fox, who sought nothing less than total control of the Cabinet, a monopoly of power which the king detested in one whom he found personally objectionable. Fox's weapon in the battle which followed the death of Rockingham, in the summer of 1782, was an unholy alliance with his old enemy, North. It was a deeply offensive and widely despised alliance, but the prize, control of the Commons and, therefore, as Fox saw it, of the government, seemed big enough to over-ride demands for consistency.

But there were flaws in Fox's logic. His ministry, the notorious Fox–North coalition, was short-lived. It was strongly opposed by the king himself, who systematically plotted its destruction, and also by Pitt, who wanted no dependence on Fox and cordially detested North. When Fox obligingly provided an issue on which Pitt and the king might appeal to the country, in the shape of a radical restructuring of the East India Company, in effect he committed political suicide. George III instructed the House of Lords to defeat the East India Bill, Pitt was placed in power, and in the spring of 1784 a general election was called.

There could be no quarrelling with the result. Fox was roundly defeated not only where the Treasury could exert its influence, but also in the larger, more open constituencies where public opinion mattered and where the popular revulsion against him was manifest. When the dust settled, Pitt was prime minister on an outstandingly secure tenure, and the Whigs were thoroughly 'dished'. Above all, reform, the hoped-for product of a hoped-for alliance between Fox and Pitt against the combined forces of George III and North, was dead – killed, it seemed, by the irresponsible antics of Fox, that 'darling of the people'.

Economic and Administrative Reform

Perhaps reform was dead anyway. Once he had nodded in the direction of his youthful principles by putting a motion for reform which he knew could not be successful without the backing of the Crown, Pitt as prime minister showed little taste for radical political activity. A reformer he proved, but not in matters affecting the constitution in Church and State. Many of the demands of the 'economical reformers' for a reduction in the corruption and waste of the court were to be carried out under Pitt. Moreover, the first, extremely hesitant steps towards free trade were taken under his guidance, notably in the commercial treaty with France in 1787.

Difficult imperial questions were also treated with a mixture of caution and innovation. The Irish had already achieved a measure of home rule. To secure their loyalty, Pitt would have given Ireland commercial equality with the mother country had the manufacturers of the Midlands and Lancashire allowed him to do so. His failure in this respect left Anglo-Irish relations in an equivocal and uncertain state. India was put to rest at least as a major issue in British politics with an East India Act which finally gave government the ultimate say in the Company's affairs, at least when they did not exclusively concern trade. In 1791 Canada, with its incursion of loyalist settlers after the American War and its intractable 'ethnic' problem in Quebec, was given a settlement which was to endure, albeit uneasily, until 1867.

In many ways, Pitt's supremacy had a very traditional appearance. He was essentially a beneficiary of the court and of the king's support. His triumph in 1784 could be made to seem as much a triumph for the Crown as anything done by a Danby or a Sunderland. The opposition to Pitt looked traditional too. Fox depended much on the heir to the throne, the future George IV, whose antics, political, financial, and sexual, were as much the despair of the king as those of any heir to the Crown before him.

But in other respects Pitt and his activities reflected the transformations of recent years. His administrative and economic reforms take their place among a great host of changes in contemporary attitudes which can easily be lost behind the political conservatism of the age. That most flourishing product of the Enlightenment mind – utility – was already in sight. Jeremy Bentham and the philosophical radicals were yet to achieve a significant breakthrough in practical politics, but the flavour which they imparted or perhaps adopted was everywhere, as was the religious influence of Evangelicalism.

The New Sensibility

The reforms which really did make an impact in this period were precisely those moral, humanitarian, pragmatic 'improvements' which delighted the Evangelical mind. John Howard's famous campaign for prison reform belonged to the 1770s and 1780s. His 'voyage of discovery' or 'Circumnavigation of Charity', in Burke's words, provided a powerful stimulus to the work of remodelling the institutions he visited and described. The Sunday Schools sprang from the same era of earnest endeavour, as did the widespread drive to establish Friendly Societies supervised by the clergy. Traditional recreations of the lower classes came increasingly under the disapproving inspection of their social superiors, particularly when, like cock-fighting and bull-baiting, they involved cruelty to animals.

There was also a distinct shift in attitudes towards imperial responsibility. Burke's campaign against Warren Hastings, the saviour of British India, proved protracted. The impeachment failed despite Hastings's apparent guilt on some of the charges. Exonerated or not, Hastings might be considered the victim of changing standards of public morality. What would have been tolerated in a Clive was tolerated no longer. The treatment of subject peoples had ceased to be a matter of indifference at home. Interest in 'uncivilized' peoples, from the Red Indians to Captain Cook's South Sea islanders, like Burke's indignation on behalf of more sophisticated but equally subjugated Asians, revealed a new sensitivity, tinged with romanticism, to the plight of the victims of empire.

The most notorious target of the new sensibility was, of course, the slave trade. The campaign, led by Granville Sharp in the formative years of the 1770s, and by William Wilberforce in the 1780s, was to wait many years before success. But there were victories along the way. In the case of James Sommersett, 1772, a Negro slave brought by a West Indian planter to London was freed on the grounds that no law of England authorized 'so high an act of dominion as slavery'. The publicity value of this decision was out of all proportion to its legal significance, but the interest which it aroused caught the essence of the late eighteenth-century mind, with its emphasis on human equality, religious redemption, and political conservatism. For Wilberforce and his friends were staunch defenders of the establishment in Church and State, and utterly uninterested in radical politics. In this they expressed the serious-minded, Evangelical enthusiasm of the business classes of the new industrial England. For all the supposedly unrepresentative nature of the political system it was these classes which Wilberforce's friend Pitt best represented. It was also their instinct for obstinate defence of the interests of property, combined with thrusting commercial aggressiveness and unlimited moral earnestness, which was to carry the England of the American War into the era of the French Revolution.

Chapter 7
Endpiece

A century after the Revolution of 1688 there was thought of celebrating its hundredth anniversary, though for some of those involved 'celebration' was not precisely the word. The failure of the reform movement of the early 1780s had left its supporters in a disillusioned frame of mind. Renewed attempts by dissenters to secure the repeal of the Test and Corporation Act were heavily defeated in Parliament. George III's attack of apparent insanity in 1788 had opened the possibility of a new Whig government under his son as prince regent. But the king's recovery in 1789 ensured the survival of Pitt's ministry and was greeted by an outburst of national relief that disheartened the opponents of the regime. Those who believed that the triumph of George III and Pitt in 1784 had turned the constitutional clock back to the days of Charles II saw little reason to rejoice in the centenary of the Revolution but considerable reason to lament its betrayal.

Defenders of the regime were more likely to praise its recent achievements than search for seventeenth-century precedents. The pace of economic growth in the 1780s confounded those who considered the loss of the 13 colonies the death knell of Britain's prosperity. The United Kingdom's diplomatic stature and influence had recovered dramatically since 1783, both on the Continent and overseas. Startling developments in France in 1788 and 1789 suggested that a long-standing enemy and rival was about to be disabled if not extinguished in both capacities. A world-wide empire of trade and dominion had recovered its vigour.

Numerous foreign observers and visitors were impressed by Britain as something of a prodigy among eighteenth-century nations. Its success defied conventional analysis of power and wealth. Most international success stories of the time had to do with the character of a ruler or the characteristics of a system of government. Britain's Georges were hardly to be compared with a Louis XIV or Frederick II. With the aid of its national debt, and apparently endless capacity to borrow from itself, the British state had demonstrated its power as a war machine. But it lacked most of the powers of the military states of the Continent and had lost ground during the preceding century when at odds with its own subjects. By any external standards the press was remarkably free. Personal liberty, on the whole, far exceeded what existed elsewhere. Religious freedom and tolerance had an older and firmer base than in most societies. The institutions of state enjoyed widespread, if not universal, support. All this suggested not a high degree of military, monarchical, or bureacratic power but a confident, albeit complacent, propertied polity.

On the eve of the French Revolution and with little sense of what it portended, it was easy for foreigners and Britons alike to see the British Isles as the site of modernity, combining economic growth, political maturity, and imperial strength on a scale unparalleled elsewhere. The humiliations of Louis XVI, compared with Louis XIV a century before, merely accentuated Britain's apparent progress, as the ruins of the Bastille threw into high relief the glories of Windsor. A sense of insecurity had been one of the most marked features of the Britain of 1689. There was little sign of it in 1789.

Further Reading

This list identifies 50 titles, selected not only to provide authoritative introductions to major topics, but also to permit the reader to sample some of the best of modern research on the period.

General

L. Colley, *Britons: Forging the Nation, 1707–1837* (New Haven CT, 1992).

S. J. Connolly, *Religion, Law and Power: The Making of Protestant Ireland* (London, 1992).

T. M. Devine, *The Scottish Nation, 1700–2000* (London, 1999).

R. F. Foster, *Modern Ireland* (London, 1988).

G. H. Jenkins, *The Foundations of Modern Wales, 1642–1780* (Oxford, 1987).

P. Langford, *A Polite and Commercial People: England 1727–1783*, New Oxford History of England (Oxford, 1989).

R. B. McDowell, *Ireland in the Age of Imperialism and Revolution 1760–1801* (Oxford, 1979).

F. O'Gorman, *The Long Eighteenth Century: British Political and Social History 1688–1832* (London, 1997).

W. Prest, *Albion Ascendant: English History, 1660–1815* (Oxford, 1998).

T. C. Smout, *A History of the Scottish People, 1560–1830* (London, 1970).

Politics and Government

J. Black, *A System of Ambition: British Foreign Policy, 1660–1793* (London, 1991).

J. Brewer, *The Sinews of Power: War, Money and the English State, 1688–1783* (London, 1989).

J. Cannon, *Parliamentary Reform 1740–1832* (Cambridge, 1982).

I. Christie, *Crisis of Empire* (London, 1976).

H. T. Dickinson, *Liberty and Property: Political Ideology in Eighteenth-Century Britain* (London, 1977).

J. Ehrman, *The Younger Pitt*, 3 vols (London, 1969–96).

F. Harris, *A Passion for Government: The Life of Sarah, Duchess of Marlborough* (Oxford, 1991).

J. R. Jones, *Britain and the World 1649–1815* (London, 1980).

P. Langford, *Public Life and the Propertied Englishman, 1689–1798* (Oxford, 1991).

L. Mitchell, *Charles James Fox* (Oxford, 1992).

F. O'Gorman, *Voters, Patrons, and Parties: The Unreformed Electoral System in Hanoverian England, 1734–1832* (Oxford, 1989).

N. Rogers, *Whigs and Cities: Popular Politics in the Age of Walpole and Pitt* (Oxford, 1989).

W. A. Speck, *Reluctant Revolutionaries* (London, 1989).

P. D. G. Thomas, *Revolution in America: Britain and the Colonies, 1763–1776* (Oxford, 1992).

P. D. G. Thomas, *Lord North* (Oxford, 1976).

P. D. G. Thomas, *John Wilkes: A Friend to Liberty* (Oxford, 1996).

Society and Economy

J. M. Beattie, *Crime and the Courts in England, 1660–1800* (Oxford, 1986).

P. Borsay, *The English Urban Renaissance: Culture and Society in the Eighteenth-Century Provincial Town, 1660–1770* (London, 1989).

J. Cannon, *Aristocratic Century: The Peerage of Eighteenth-Century England* (Cambridge, 1984).

P. Corfield, *Power and the Professions in Britain 1700–1850* (London, 1995).

M. Daunton, *Progress and Poverty: An Economic and Social History of Britain 1700–1850* (Oxford, 1995).

V. Gatrell, *The Hanging Tree: Execution and the English Public, 1770–1868* (Oxford, 1994).

D. Hay and N. Rogers, *Eighteenth-Century English Society: Shuttles and Swords* (Oxford, 1997).

P. Hudson, *The Industrial Revolution* (London, 1992).

R. Porter, *English Society in the Eighteenth Century* (London, 1963).

H. D. Rack, *Reasonable Enthusiast: John Wesley and the Rise of Methodism* (Oxford, 1989).

R. Sweet, *The English Town, 1680–1740: Government, Society and Culture* (Harlow, 1999).

E. P. Thompson, *Customs in Common* (London, 1991).

Religion, Ideas, and Culture

J. Brewer, *The Pleasures of the Imagination: England in the Eighteenth Century* (London, 1997).

A. C. Chitnis, *The Scottish Enlightenment: A Social History* (Edinburgh, 1976).

W. Gibson, *Church, State and Society, 1760–1850* (London, 1994).

D. Hempton, *Religion and Political Culture in Britain and Ireland: From the Glorious Revolution to the Decline of Empire* (Cambridge, 1996).

R. W. Malcolmson, *Popular Recreations in English Society, 1700–1850* (Cambridge, 1973).

P. J. Marshall, *The Great Map of Mankind: British Perceptions of the World in the Age of Enlightenment* (London, 1982).

E. G. Rupp, *Religion in England, 1688–1791* (Oxford, 1986).

L. Stone, *The Family, Sex and Marriage in England, 1500–1800* (London, 1977).

K. Thomas, *Man and the Natural World: Changing Attitudes in England, 1500–1800* (London, 1983).

J. Uglow, *Hogarth: A Life and a World* (London, 1997).

M. Watts, *The Dissenters: From the Reformation to the French Revolution* (London, 1978).

A. Vickery, *The Gentleman's Daughter: Women's Lives in Georgian England* (New Haven CT, 1998).

The English Satirical Print 1600–1823, 7 vols (Cambridge, 1986).

Chronology

1688	James II's son born; William of Orange invades: James II takes flight, accession of William III (of Orange) and Mary
1689	Bill of Rights settles succession to the throne and declares illegal various grievances; Toleration Act grants rights to Trinitarian Protestant dissenters
1690	Battle of the Boyne: William III defeats Irish and French army
1694	Bank of England founded; death of Queen Mary; Triennial Act sets the maximum duration of a Parliament at three years
1695	Lapse of Licensing Act
1697	Peace treaty of Ryswick between allied powers of the League of Augsburg and France; Civil List Act votes funds for the maintenance of the royal household
1701	War of Spanish Succession begins; Act of Settlement settles the royal succession on the descendants of Sophia of Hanover
1702	Death of William III; accession of Anne
1704	Battle of Blenheim: British, Dutch, German and Austrian troops defeat French and Bavarian forces; British capture of Gibraltar from Spain
1707	Union of England and Scotland
1710	Impeachment of Dr Sacheverell; ministry of Robert Harley
1713	Peace treaty of Utrecht concludes the War of Spanish Succession
1714	Death of Anne; accession of George I

1715	Jacobite rebellion aimed at overthrowing the Hanoverian succession fails
1716	Septennial Act sets the maximum duration of a Parliament at seven years
1717	Whig split; suspension of convocation
1720	South Sea Bubble: many investors ruined after speculation in the stock of the South Sea Company
1721	Ministry of Robert Walpole
1722	Atterbury Plot, notable Jacobite plot
1726	Jonathan Swift's *Gulliver's Travels* published
1727	Death of George I; accession of George II
1729	Alexander Pope's *Dunciad* published
1730	Walpole/Townshend split
1733	Excise crisis: Walpole has to abandon his plans to reorganize the customs and excise
1737	Death of Queen Caroline
1738	John Wesley's 'conversion' experience
1739	War of Jenkins' Ear with Spain
1740	War of Austrian Succession
1741	Samuel Richardson's *Pamela* published
1742	Fall of Walpole
1743	Ministry of Henry Pelham
1745	Jacobite rebellion
1746	Battle of Culloden: Cumberland routs the Jacobite army
1748	Peace of Aix-la-Chapelle concludes War of Austrian Succession
1752	Adoption of Gregorian calendar
1753	Jewish Naturalization Bill
1754	Ministry of Newcastle
1756	Seven Years War: Britain allied with Frederick the Great of Prussian against France, Austria, and Russia
1757	Ministry of William Pitt and Newcastle; victory of Plassey
1759	Capture of Quebec from French
1760	Death of George II; accession of George III
1761	Laurence Sterne's *Tristram Shandy* published

1762	Bute's ministry
1763	Peace of Paris concludes Seven Years War; ministry of George Grenville; John Wilkes and general warrants
1765	Ministry of Rockingham; American Stamp tax
1766	Ministry of Chatham
1768	Ministry of Grafton; Middlesex election crisis
1769	James Watt's steam engine patented
1770	Lord North's ministry; Edmund Burke's *Thoughts on the Present Discontents* published; Falkland Islands crisis
1773	Boston Tea Party
1774	Coercive Acts passed in retaliation for Boston Tea Party
1776	Declaration of American Independence; Edward Gibbon's *Decline and Fall* and Adam Smith's *Wealth of Nations* published
1779	Christopher Wyvill's Association movement
1780	Gordon Riots against the Catholic Relief Act
1781	American victory at Yorktown
1782	Second Rockingham ministry
1783	Ministry of Shelburne; Peace of Versailles recognizes independence of American colonies; Fox–North coalition; younger Pitt's ministry
1784	East India Act
1785	Pitt's motion for parliamentary reform defeated
1786	Eden commercial treaty with France
1788	Regency crisis
1789	French Revolution

Prime Ministers 1721–89

Robert Walpole	Apr. 1721
Earl of Wilmington	Feb. 1741
Henry Pelham	Aug. 1743
Duke of Newcastle	Mar. 1754
Duke of Devonshire	Nov. 1756
Duke of Newcastle	July 1757
Earl of Bute	May 1762
George Grenville	Apr. 1763
Marquess of Rockingham	July 1765
Earl of Chatham	July 1766
Duke of Grafton	Oct. 1768
Lord North	Jan. 1770
Marquess of Rockingham	Mar. 1782
Earl of Shelburne	July 1782
Duke of Portland	Apr. 1783
William Pitt	Dec. 1783

Index

Page numbers in *italics* refer to illustrations or captions. There may also be textual references on the same page.

Index

113

Visit the
VERY SHORT
INTRODUCTIONS
Web site

www.oup.co.uk/vsi

➤ **Information** about all published titles

➤ News of **forthcoming books**

➤ **Extracts** from the books, including titles not yet published

➤ **Reviews** and views

➤ **Links** to other **web sites** and main OUP web page

➤ Information about **VSIs in translation**

➤ **Contact** the editors

➤ **Order** other **VSIs** on-line